THIS BOOK IS DEDICATED
IN MEMORY OF

JIM FYFFE
(1945-2003)

THROUGH THE EYES OF A TIGER©
A BOOK BY AUBURN FANS... FOR AUBURN FANS!

Mark Stanfield • Tim Stanfield • Illia Ayers • David Kessler

Published by:

FANtastic Memories, L.L.C.
P. O. Box 660582
Birmingham, AL 35266
www.4au2.com • info@4au2.com

Edited by Amy Wright and Carol Muse Evans, Auburn Class of 1985.

Cover and Design by Atticus Communications, LLC

ISBN: 0-9740245-8-9

First Printing: August 2003

Printed in U.S.A.

THROUGH THE EYES OF A TIGER©

A BOOK BY AUBURN FANS…
FOR AUBURN FANS!

Mark Stanfield • Tim Stanfield •
Illia Ayers • David Kessler

First Edition

"Auburn vs. Alabama - November 22, 1997"
David Housel and Tim Stanfield

FOREWORD

"Of the People, By the People, For the People..."

For 227 years that phrase has been used to describe the American idea, the American Dream...

Now it can be used to describe Auburn, this book about Auburn...

"Of the People, By the People, For the People..." That is what this book is all about.

"Of the Auburn People, By the Auburn People, For the Auburn People..."

In other words, "If you ain't Auburn, you don't want to buy this book–unless you are trying to understand the Auburn people or are buying it for an Auburn person. If those are your reasons, it is money well spent.

The stories herein help explain and articulate why Auburn is special. It is a glimpse into the heart and soul of the Auburn people, the Auburn Nation, some of the things we hold dear and true. It is a story of Auburn people, written by Auburn people for Auburn people. Nothing more; nothing less. That is more than enough.

The oral tradition is an important part of our culture. Stories and traditions, legend and lore, have been passed down from generation to generation. Much of what we know about our past, as a nation, as people, as a culture, we know from the storytelling tradition.

We weren't there when the Declaration of Independence was signed in 1776 and we weren't there when Auburn defeated Georgia 10-0 in 1892, that long ago day when college football as we know it came to the Deep South... We weren't there in 1942 when Monk Gafford and a band of determined, dedicated Tigers, who believed in themselves and their destiny, upset Rose Bowl-bound Georgia 27-13 in Columbus... We weren't there when Auburn beat Alabama 14-13 in 1949, sparking a "feather-storm" over Birmingham's Legion Field, and some of us, believe it or not, were not there on Dec. 2, 1989, the First-Time-Ever Game. But we know about it. We know what it was like to be there. We know because of the stories and memories of those who were there, the stories and memories that were passed down to us. Put together, they make us what we are today.

This book, "Through the Eyes of a Tiger," is truly a book "By Auburn Fans, For Auburn Fans..." Auburn People, telling Auburn stories, about the moments and the memories that were special to us in our time, in our day. It is an important part of sharing the Auburn story and the Auburn tradition–who we are–with the Auburn Men and Women yet to come–the Auburn Men and Women of tomorrow who will make Auburn what it will become.

These are our stories, stories worth retelling and worth remembering... They have made us who we are...

War Eagle!

War Eagle, Forever! And Ever!

David Housel
Athletic Director
Auburn University

"WAR EAGLE"
Photo submitted by Cathy Henry

FANtastic Memories, LLC
"Auburn vs. Ole Miss - September 8, 2001"
Tim Stanfield, Illia Ayers, Mark Stanfield and David Kessler

INTRODUCTION

As faithful supporters of Auburn University, we all know that Tigers come in many shapes and sizes. There are so many elements encompassing our lovely Village on the Plains that generate tremendous pride. Through the Eyes of a Tiger© is a reflection of these elements as seen through the eyes of individual Auburn fans.

We have seen and read wonderful books by coaches, players, and well-respected dignitaries of the Auburn community. However, we wanted to create a literary conduit revealing the unique perspectives and experiences of the tried and true Auburn fans. We have attempted to capture the essence of what it means to be an Auburn Tiger and to experience life within the Auburn Family.

Our goal was to achieve tailgating in book form, featuring short stories and essays "By Auburn Fans... For Auburn Fans." We requested that Auburn fans put their favorite experiences into words. This book features fifty authors, ranging from friends and family to fellow fans we have met at games, Auburn Clubs, random encounters, and via our website www.4AU2.com. We have also taken this opportunity to share a few of our own favorite memories. Since this project began in April 2001, we have received hundreds of written submissions from fourteen states and two countries.

Recognizing that we are neither professional writers nor editors, this project has been a challenging labor of love. We sincerely hope you will enjoy the stories you read in Through the Eyes of a Tiger©. We also encourage you to submit your favorite Auburn memories for future editions so that your experiences will be enjoyed by others.

It's Great to be an Auburn Tiger!

FANtastic Memories, LLC

THANK YOU

Thank you for buying Through the Eyes of a Tiger©. We offer our gratitude to the individuals and organizations that contributed to the production of this book, making our dream a reality.

We sincerely thank the Auburn faithful that believed in our project and submitted their stories. We received hundreds of stories throughout the country and abroad. We truly wanted this project to be "A Book By Auburn Fans… For Auburn Fans," and with your help we have accomplished this goal. Although every story could not be included, we are saving all submissions and accepting new material for future editions.

We extend our gratitude to those that directly contributed to the production of this book. **Atticus Communication (Miles Wright '90, Shawn Wright '85, and Vic Wheeler '84)** contributed their expertise in design, layout and production. **Amy Wright** provided first line editing and creative content. **Carol Muse Evans '85** contributed with editing, creative content and proofreading. These individuals are members of the Auburn family, and champions in our eyes.

We appreciate the businesses and individuals that have materially supported our infant company, FANtastic Memories, LLC. In doing so, they have made this book financially feasible. We have listed these special contributors at the conclusion of the book and on our website www.4AU2.com. Please support these businesses, as they have supported this effort.

We are also thankful for the true inspiration behind this book, **Auburn University**. This great institution is the tie that binds the Auburn Family. As a representative of the University, we extend our appreciation to **David Housel**. Since our first discussion with David, he has been a great coach and cheerleader for the development of this project.

We thank our respective families and friends, who have offered tremendous support to our dream of creating this book. Since April 2001, they have sacrificed a great deal of quality time as we planned and prepared this project. We appreciate their sacrifice, words of encouragement, and their influence in our lives. We are thankful that they believe in this book as much as we do.

With that said… in the words of the late Leland Childs…

…*"Heeerrrre Come The Tigers!"*

Thanks & WAR EAGLE!!!

FANtastic Memories, LLC

DISCLAIMER

TABLE OF CONTENTS

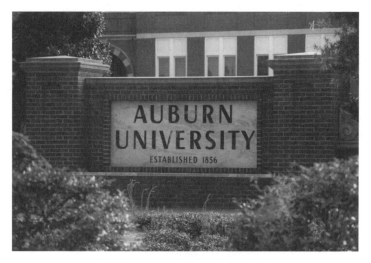

"Welcome to Auburn University"
Photo submitted by Cathy Henry

"Visit the University Chapel and give thanks to God for the opportunity you have. For every student at Auburn, there are many others who wish they could be there."

– Glenn Mizell

YOUR FIRST DAY AT AUBURN...

Walk up to the corner of Glenn Avenue and College Street. Walk south along College Street towards Magnolia Avenue, past the shops and restaurants you will frequent during your time at Auburn.

Stop by Toomer's Drugstore on the northeast corner of College Street and Magnolia Avenue, order a small lemonade and look across Toomer's corner at the University. Think to yourself; the education I'll receive in these buildings will form my future.

Pause for a brief moment of reflection, as you continue walking south along College Street, stop by J&M Bookstore and look at the AU stuff in there. Someday, you'll have some of that stuff for yourself and wear it with pride.

Continue down College Street until you reach Smith Hall. Take a moment to sit down on the steps and look at Samford Park. Try to visualize all of the students who have gone before you. They have helped to make Auburn what it is today.

Visit the University Chapel and give thanks to God for the opportunity you have. For every student at Auburn, there are many others who wish they could be there.

Cross College Street, continue west along Thatch Avenue and pay a visit to the Ralph Brown Draughon Library. Realize

1

you'll spend countless hours in this building expanding your mind and developing your skills.

From the Library, look south towards Comer Hall and remember that Auburn's agricultural heritage is one of its greatest strengths. Others who do not understand Auburn often ridicule the University over lunch or dinner. You must never let these people distract you, for they are too small-minded to realize that the food they put in their mouths is the direct result of the work done at Auburn.

Continue walking west until you reach the lawn in front of Cater Hall. During the spring and summer, you'll probably pass some time between classes sitting here, enjoying a quite moment and thinking about who you are, where you've been and where you're going.

Keep walking west to the concourse next to Haley Center. Look to your right, and you will see Broun Hall and other engineering buildings. Realize that, at that moment, the people in those buildings are designing the tools and machinery that will make our lives better in the future.

Walking south you will see the complex of science buildings, and beyond them is Dudley Hall and Telfair Peet Theater. You may stop in sometime and see a play. You never know, the actor/actress may be on television or in the movies someday.

From Roosevelt Drive, turn right and walk west past Jordan-Hare Stadium and Plainsman Park. It's where you'll spend many fall Saturdays and see many exciting games. There's no doubt that athletics are a big part of the Auburn experience, but it's just one part of the complete Auburn experience that is so dear to the hearts and minds of all graduates. It is this total experience that makes us successful, dedicated and makes us a family.

Continue west, cross Donahue Drive and see Beard-Eaves Memorial Coliseum. When it's your turn, you'll graduate in this building. It is the last place you'll be a student at Auburn.

Many of us made that same trek on our first day at Auburn and on many days after that. Though Auburn is a large campus, it immediately felt like a small town. We knew that we would meet wonderful people here, and we knew those friendships would last a lifetime.

Would your first day at Auburn be complete without this walk? Not really. You see, as a student, you are the future of Auburn. And all those who have gone before trust you to take this walk, to understand its' significance, and see it through to the end. Rest assured that we will welcome you "to the other side" when you have completed it.

Congratulations on your decision to attend Auburn and welcome to our family.

Glenn Mizell
Brentwood, Tennessee
Auburn University
Class of 1988

Tim and Mark Stanfield
October 24, 1976

"A 'Double Day' (coined by my great friend, Michael DeFore) is when Auburn wins and Alabama loses. I often wondered whom we cheered for more, Auburn, or whoever was playing Alabama that Saturday. The only thing that could even come close to offsetting the sinking feeling of an Auburn loss was an Alabama loss later the same day."

– Mark Stanfield

TIGER AT BIRTH
"Growing Up in Our House"

Growing up in our house, you were taught to be a huge Auburn Football fan, no questions asked. Circling your hand in the air and chanting, "WARRRRRR EAGLE!" was perfected by age two. Memorizing the starting offense and defense followed soon thereafter. Next came the new recruit quiz, complete with all the details: name, high school, position, key stats, hometown and what other colleges and universities had failed to land this superior young talent.

Growing up in our house, the outside world ceased to exist on game day. The late Jim Fyffe's voice could be heard bellowing throughout the house in the early morning hours. On the Saturdays that we were not heading to the Plains, the family room was carefully transformed into a makeshift stadium, complete with TV, radio, headphones, newspapers, AU programs, media guides, recruiting guides, shakers, footballs, refreshments, etc. My dad would pace incessantly. He was so deep in thought, if you asked him his name, he would have to search for the answer.

And during this time, the TV was a shrine. No one ever walked in front of the shrine on game day, not even during commercials. If you had to go to the bathroom, you held it, slithered along the floor under the line of sight or took the long way around. If the phone rang, my dad would yell, "Who would call during the Auburn game?"

Growing up in our house, it was wise to avoid mentioning "the other school" (The University of Alabama at Tuscaloosa). Our dad carefully scrutinized our childhood friends to determine their allegiance. If they were somehow misguided into believing there was actually a legitimate reason to root for "the other school," it was just because they were too young to know any better. If you happened to leave an inferior T-shirt or cup at our house, you'd never see it again. It would mysteriously turn up in a landfill somewhere, but definitely not in one piece.

Growing up in our house, Tuscaloosa was simply not a place you visited. Trips to Tuscaloosa were infrequent, to say the least, and only if absolutely necessary. When our fourth grade class took a field trip to the Bear Bryant Museum, my dad protested. It was pretty much an unspoken rule that, even if we were offered a full scholarship to Alabama, it was to be turned down.

Growing up in our house, crimson or anything resembling crimson was considered sacrilegious. My dad never owned anything crimson, not even red, for that matter. No red tie, car, sweater, cup, cap or even a toothbrush.

Growing up in our house, many people who were hated by "the other school's" fans found favor in my dad's eyes. My dad pointed out that some certain qualities of Gene Jelks were pleasing. For a few years, my dad thought Coach Bill Curry was a pretty good guy, too. Maybe it had something to do with his career record versus Auburn. Dad loved to point out the two classy, overweight guys at the Alabama games with the toilet paper rolls and Tide box on a stick. He agreed with me when I pointed out the resemblance of Coach Mike DuBose to Elmer Fudd. And Dad always loved hearing the whining, futile wishes of all the Bama fans for the return of "The Bear."

Growing up in our house, we learned definitions for words that couldn't be found in any dictionary:

A "**Double Day**" (coined by my great friend, Michael DeFore) is when Auburn wins and Alabama loses. I often wondered whom we cheered for more, Auburn, or whoever was playing Alabama that Saturday. The only thing that could even come close to offsetting the sinking feeling of an Auburn loss was an Alabama loss later the same day.

"**The Sell-Out**" is a fan that sells their tickets in the AU section to the opposing team. This could also be termed "The Benedict Arnold" or traitor. There is nothing more uncomfortable than sitting with 15,000 of your fellow AU fans in the AU section at the LA Coliseum but having two USC fans behind you, seated next to an AU Alum that is asking you to sit down for the kickoff. If ever caught in this dilemma, it is better to "take-one-for-the-team" and eat the cost of the ticket, rather than spoil a great day for a fellow comrade. In addition, you are filling one of our seats with one of their fans. The only exception is if the enemy is accompanied by an AU fan and is a relative or very close friend that is pre-warned of the consequences of their decision to enter the Tiger's lair. (Note: There is nothing wrong with an AU fan buying tickets in the opposing teams section at a home or away game, just to get into the game.)

An "**Auburn Comrade**" is a fellow Auburn fan in close range in enemy territory (an Auburn away game). This comrade can be someone you have never seen before in your life and be 10 rows away. But when you are sitting in "Death Valley," "Sanford Stadium," "The Iron Bowl," "The Swamp," etc., you can look up to find this comrade... maybe he or she is a bank president and you are a truck driver... but just from the look in his or her eye, you realize at that moment this person is as close as a brother or sister.

A "State Fan" is one that is for Auburn and Alabama, but pulls for Auburn when they play Alabama. We were taught that these fair-weather fans were not the truest of Auburn fans. This is merely a feeble attempt to sit on the fence and try to avoid making enemies.

A "Blended Marriage" is in the same category as a "State Fan" and includes an Auburn husband and Bama wife, or vice-versa. You've seen the tags on the front of cars that are split down the middle. We always felt sorry for the Auburn fan in this marriage. This is a sign that true love does conquer all.

The "Conference Booster" is closely related to the "State Fan" and "Blended Marriage." An example of a "Conference Booster" is a person who thinks that if Florida wins the National Championship, it's good for the whole S.E.C. In our house, this was kind of like kissing your sister. Even though this scenario might put a few more dollars in Auburn's pockets, you could still never root for the enemy.

Growing up in our house may have been a little different than growing up in your house. It may even appear our house was a little extreme. Auburn winning wasn't everything. It was the only thing. The thought of winning was what kept us from going into a complete tailspin. It's what helped us regain our enthusiasm the following week around Wednesday in anticipation of the next Saturday's game. Honestly, it consumed us.

Overall, I think I have adjusted okay. For example, I still know the proper order for life's priorities are God, Family, Country and Auburn Football. I also know that if I had not grown up in our house, I would not be able to say that to this day: "There is nothing like that Christmas-morning tingle I get every time game day rolls around and I get to enjoy the experience of yet another 'Double Day!'"

WAR EAGLE!

Mark Stanfield
Birmingham, Alabama

Wayne Stanfield with Terry Beasley

"Auburn fans may not be able to tell you what year JFK was assassinated or what year man landed on the moon but they know the punts were blocked in 1972."

— Wayne Stanfield

DESTINY REVISITED

"Auburn vs. Alabama – December 2, 1972"

December 2, 1972, was a day of destiny for an amazing bunch of Auburn football players. It was also a day of destiny for a fan and his wife who managed to walk in the game free. I've always felt deep down inside that the football miracle might not have happened if I was not there to witness this extraordinary game. Is that crazy or what?

I was not looking forward to Auburn football as I usually did, as the long hot summer of 1972 melted away. August arrived, and a bleak September approached, and I still was unexcited about football this particular year. Why?

It was pretty simple. No Pat Sullivan, no Terry Beasley, no Heisman Trophy winning quarterback, Number 7, the best to ever line up under center at Auburn, leading the tigers down the field. No human highlight film, no blazing Number 88, the embodiment of all things great about the Auburn Spirit.

How could we go on? How could we replace two legends, two all-Americans, proclaimed the greatest by the likes of Bear Bryant and Vince Dooley? We couldn't. We would have to figure out a new way to win, somehow. You don't replace legends with more legends the next year... not at Auburn, anyway. We do replace them with players that give everything they've got and refuse to quit... players that, maybe lacking great ability, but possess that one trait that allows them to rise to greatness. In their hearts, they've got the Auburn Spirit.

The new set of leaders that would emerge in the fall of 1972 was not an awe-inspiring group. Randy Walls, our new quarterback, might have been the poster boy for slow. Terry Henley our brash running back, would carry the ball 15 times in a row in the win over 'Ole Miss. He announced to all when the huddle broke each play where he was coming with the ball. The defense was led by a 160-pound defensive back, David Langner, who thought he was a 235-pound linebacker.

The season began with four lackluster wins over Mississippi State, Tennessee-Chattanooga, Tennessee and Ole Miss. They were ugly, but wins, just the same. The overachieving Tigers were 4-0 when they traveled to Baton Rouge to meet LSU in Death Valley. LSU, with its All-American quarterback Bert Jones, the "Ruston Rifle," leading the way, dealt the Tigers a confidence-crushing loss of 35-7. Surely this would mark the end of the gutsy run the team had strung together. This bunch of guys with hearts much larger than their talent would still be fondly remembered anyway for doing the best they could have done. But for some unknown reason, these guys didn't pack it in. They continued to play hard and miraculously put together wins over Georgia Tech, Florida State, Florida and Georgia. Truly this had been a magical season. To go 8-2 losing only to LSU and a great Alabama team would be a very proud accomplishment.

To have to play the vaunted Crimson Tide 10 and 0, ranked Number 2 in the nation, averaging almost 400 yards and 40 points a game, was not going to be a very fitting end to an otherwise fairy tale season. The Tide was rolling into Birmingham as a 15-point favorite, looking to crush us on their way to a national championship.

Some of my friends laughed when I called them early in the week and said I actually thought we had a chance. I tried to fire them up, telling them we owed it to this team to get behind them in a big way. Personally, this team had really inspired me with the way it fought. I would be going to the game, somehow, some way, even though I didn't have a ticket or any decent prospects of getting one.

On Friday Afternoon, I sneaked away from my job at a downtown bank and drove out to Legion Field to watch the Auburn team work out. Alabama was already on the field and laughing as they casually warmed up. They were definitely not concerned about the upcoming game. John Hannah, their All-American lineman, looked gigantic in his sweat suit. He was taking snaps at quarterback and throwing short passes to guys trying to catch the ball behind their backs.

When Auburn came out in their navy sweats and helmets, they seemed much more serious and business-like. I was struck by the contrast of the two teams warming up. I thought Auburn seemed to have a quiet determination as they worked out. Was I mistaking determination for intimidation?

I may have had $30 when I left with my wife to arrive at Legion Field at 9 a.m. on game day. I began searching high and low for tickets with no success. The $30 I was offering only drew snickers from the scalpers. Around 1:15 p.m.... before the 1:30 p.m. kickoff, I was basically a beaten man, realizing I was not going to get into the game. As I headed around the stadium back to my car, I saw one of my brother's friends who said my brother had something for me at gate 1. When I ran to gate 1 to meet him, he had an unused Alabama – LSU ticket from earlier in the season. Guess what? It was the same color and size as the Auburn - Alabama ticket. I thought anything was possible.

My brother and his wife had their two tickets. My wife and my brother's wife got in line with my brother behind them.

When they got to the ticket taker they pointed to him and said he's got the tickets. They walked in and he handed them two tickets. Three people on two tickets! My wife was in free! I gained new confidence that I could get in on my bogus ticket. My ticket was for the horseshoe end of the stadium. There were two long lines for two ticket takers. When I handed him my ticket upside down, he tore the stub off and handed it to me. I was in!

My wife was in the upper deck, and I was downstairs. I told her I'd meet her at halftime. When we met, I helped her scale a small fence, and we were together at last. I had spent the first half in an Alabama section and didn't intend to go back there for the second half. We made our way right to the middle of the largest section of Auburn faithful. She managed to squeeze in on the end of a row, and I sat in the aisle beside her.

The first half had not offered much hope if you were an Auburn fan. We were lucky to only be down 9-0. The only highlight was Roger Mitchell blocking an extra point attempt. No one knew the importance of this at that time. (On a side note, 17 years later, while tailgating before the 1989 Auburn – Alabama game at Auburn, I was introduced to Roger Mitchell's sister. She probably thought I was a little crazy when I had her sign my hat, "Roger Mitchell's sister.")

Several things stick out in my mind about the second half. One rowdy older Auburn fan kept holding up a battery-powered monkey that would bang two cymbals together. The man would say, "Listen to the bear, listen to the bear." This seemed to anger the younger, arrogant Alabama fans seated directly in front of him.

I remember hearing the murmur of booing when Coach Ralph "Shug" Jordan elected to have Gardner Jett kick a field goal to make it 16 – 3. It was fourth and eight, and the crowd wanted to go for it. The man with the monkey stood up and loudly proclaimed, "It's going to be 17-16, 17-16," much to the disdain and laughter of the fans in front of him. When the first block and touchdown occurred, it was exhilarating! We had finally done something to fire up the team and the crowd. It was now 16-10. I think everyone thought, deep in the recesses of their minds, that if we could stop them again, something could happen.

When Mike Neel crashed Terry Davis to the turf on a third and four, everyone knew they would have to punt. Maybe they could fumble the snap, maybe it would be a bad punt, maybe we could run it back, maybe get good field position and try a couple of "Hail Marys." Anything could happen! Anything but another blocked punt. Blocking adjustments would be made and the crowd would gasp as we would come close, but he would get it off. We'd try a couple of unsuccessful long passes, and the game would be over.

The ball was snapped to the punter... a good snap... and he had it. Then time stood still for an instant, God rolled time back and the same thing happened just exactly as before. The same little Bill Newton from Fayette was bursting through the line and smothering Greg Gantt's punt. The same David Langer was catching it on the run and running across the goal. Maybe I was dreaming, but wasn't that Gardner Jett running off the field, and didn't the scoreboard say 17-16?

I struggled to get up from the floor of the stands where the unknown fat lady I was hugging and I had fallen. I made my way to the wall at the bottom of our section pulling my wife behind me. I stood there for what seemed like an eternity as the last moment ticked away. When David Langner intercepted the pass and dropped to his knees, it was over.

There were no strangers. Everyone was hugging, laughing and crying in jubilation. We had just witnessed the most shocking five minutes in the history of football. The Alabama – LSU ticket I had gotten in on became a good luck piece that I would pull out of my wallet in the future when an Auburn team needed a big play.

I lost that good luck piece during the 1994 Auburn Tiger walk at Starkville, Mississippi. I had my kids search the ground for an hour before giving up. It had meant a lot to me. However we won that game and knocked off Number 1 Florida in Gainesville the next week as I watched.

From time to time, I think back to that day. Three things always happen when I do. I smile, a little shiver goes down the back of my neck and I have to wipe away a little moisture from the corners of my eyes. Auburn fans may not be able to tell you what year President John F. Kennedy was assassinated or what year man landed on the moon, but they know the punts were blocked in 1972.

Anyway, that's my story, and I'm sticking to it. I've told it for 30 years, and I'll keep on telling it until I'm gone. Then my kids will tell their kids. Yes, I'll continue to revisit that day often… that "Day of Destiny."

Wayne Stanfield
Birmingham, Alabama
Auburn University
Class of 1969

"Auburn vs. Southern California"
Los Angeles, California - September 2, 2002
Back Row: Jeff Mimbs, Tim Stanfield, Wayne Stanfield
and Tommy Barton. Front Row: David Kessler,
Scott Stanfield and Mark Stanfield

Auburn University Chapel
Photo submitted by Cathy Henry

*"As the game reached the final moments, time
stood still as the angelic Frank Sanders lifted his
wings for the defining catch of the game. The
enemy had been silenced 36-33. ... The Auburn
flag had been thrust into the ground, "The
Swamp" waters parted, and we were delivered
safely back to that Promised Land on the Plains."*

– Illia Ayers

THE CONVERSION
"Baptism in The Swamp – October 15, 1994"

Growing up in a state where football and religion run in close circles was difficult in a family suffering from DFFS (Dysfunctional Football Fan Syndrome). My father attended the University of Tennessee, and my stepfather attended the University of Alabama. Luckily, the Tullahoma School of Cosmetology, where my mother attended, did not have a football program.

Nevertheless, one could imagine my dilemma. For many years, I struggled through the land of the lost (football team allegiance, that is). This all changed in 1994 on the weekend of my conversion. Faithful Auburn brothers and sisters, I would like to share my testimony with you.

In 1994, I enrolled in Auburn University. I must admit that my allegiance to Auburn was somewhat undefined until my Auburn friends convinced me to make what they termed a "pilgrimage," a pilgrimage to "The Swamp."

It is often told that sharing a common enemy makes for a strong relationship. I shared this common enemy with my Auburn friends in the Florida Gators.

The Gators were rolling with the hopes of a Terry Dean Heisman and a Steve Spurrier National Championship. The distinctly-Yankee tone of "Go Gators" and "Gator Bait" filled the air from the time we arrived. I prayed that this obnoxious display from the carnival workforce capitol would cease.

As a 17-point underdog, the Tigers' chances seemed slim, but I couldn't help noticing the humble confidence displayed by the Auburn faithful. It reminded me of David versus Goliath from the Old Testament. Only this time, the masses did not tremble in the presence of the enemy. As the "Jaws" theme music (which, of course, has nothing to do with a Gator) belted from the Gator Band, the Auburn fans did not waver, but grew stronger and stronger as the moment of truth neared.

The Tigers on the field displayed this confidence and determination in action, taking early blows, but never losing faith. There seemed to be divine intervention that day, as several seemingly inevitable Gator scoring attempts were thwarted. The defense was truly inspired, intercepting countless passes to keep Auburn in the game. The offense contributed when it counted, pressing Florida to the final wire.

As the game reached the final moments, time stood still as the angelic Frank Sanders lifted his wings for the defining catch of the game. The enemy had been silenced 36-33.

My baptism in "The Swamp" was complete. I was now part of a new family. As we left the stadium, I stood in awe of the spectacle that I had witnessed. I found a great faith and love for my Alma Mater that day. I truly experienced a change of heart. I thank my friends for leading me to the truth. The Auburn flag had been thrust into the ground, "The Swamp" waters parted, and we were delivered safely back to that Promised Land on the Plains.

War Eagle and Amen!

Illia Ayers
Birmingham, Alabama
AuburnUniversity
Class of 1997

"My AU Cheerleader"
Mark & Katie Stanfield

L-R: Mark Stanfield, Ginny Dowdy, Mark Harless, James Dowdy,
Carol Dowdy, Jamie Benson and David Kessler

*"There are always all kinds of tall tales and urban
legends floating around about the crazy things
Auburn fans have done in order to make it to
'the big game.' However, James A. Dowdy, Sr.
might just have the best story of them all.
But it's no tall tale. It's pure truth when he
says he made a 70-mile, round-trip journey
on a bicycle to see the Tigers play."*

*– Excerpt from Amy Wright interview
with James A. Dowdy, Sr.*

THE LEGENDARY RIDE
FOR PRIDE

As remembered by James A. Dowdy, Sr.
Written by Amy Wright

There are always all kinds of tall tales and urban legends floating around about the crazy things Auburn fans have done in order to make it to "the big game." However, James A. Dowdy, Sr. might just have the best story of them all. But it's no tall tale. It's pure truth when he says he made a 70-mile, round-trip journey on a bicycle to see the Tigers play.

"It was either 1941 or 1942," recalls the 84-year-old, self-proclaimed, lifelong Auburn fan. "It was the year Georgia won the Rose Bowl. Their only loss that year was to Auburn. I remember it like it was yesterday."

"The game was in Columbus, Georgia, and we wanted to go, but we didn't have any money," Dowdy continues. "But what we did have was manpower. There were five or six of us. So we decided to ride. That's right… we rode our bikes. Seems like we left when the moon was still up. All I know is that it was early in the morning. It was 35 miles and uphill all the way. On the way there, the team buses passed us and we cheered them on as we kept peddling. It wasn't easy but we got to see the game. And what a game it was!"

"They had three All-Americans," Dowdy continues. "Our outstanding player was Monk Gafford from Sandy Ridge, a running back. Well, they knocked him out, and he had to go to the sidelines. That really riled the fans up. Gafford was pretty banged up and they didn't want to put him back in. But, despite what the trainers said, he came back in, and Auburn won the game 27-13. It was an extra-special effort on the part of the Auburn team. And it was one of the most exciting games I've ever seen. I'd take that 70-mile round trip ride again today to see a game that exciting."

Dowdy does note that he and his fellow peddlers didn't make the trip back to Auburn that evening, but stayed with some friends and hopped back on their bikes for the return trip the next morning. Mr. Dowdy did say, "If you ever want to go to Columbus, Georgia, just get yourself a three-speed bike."

That amazing ride for pride back in the 1940s was actually just one extremely noteworthy example of Dowdy's lifelong career as a loyal Tiger follower. As a student… Dowdy enrolled in Auburn in 1939… he obviously made somewhat superhuman efforts to be in the stands when the orange and blue were on the field. But this commitment to the Tigers has never wavered.

"I have an outstanding record of attending Auburn games," Dowdy says, proudly. "I went to the games with a friend of mine, Marvin Marianna, who had gone to 345 consecutive games. My buddy actually went on a stretcher one time. He also learned to fly so we could go. It was fun. I still get down there today. I wouldn't miss it. For many years I drove to all the games in a motor home, going on Thursday to get our spot. During the 2002 season, we rented a four-bedroom apartment so our family could enjoy the whole weekend at Auburn."

Dowdy explained that he got his love of Auburn from his father who went to Auburn after serving in World War I. "I also had four children, three in-laws and three grandchildren who've gone to Auburn. When my youngest daughter told me she wanted to go to Alabama, I told her she could... if she paid her own way. She didn't go to Alabama and thanks me every day."

"Truth is, I plan on dying and going to Auburn," Dowdy laughs, finally adding that he is just kidding.

James A. Dowdy, Sr.
Birmingham, Alabama
Auburn University
Class of 1943

Tim Stanfield, Dr. Gregg Carr and Mark Stanfield

*"Auburn fans, always know that your voices are
heard and your support is truly inspiring to the
many athletes that have competed in the past and
will compete in the future. You make a difference.
For that, I thank you and now join in your cause."*

*– Dr. Gregg Carr
Auburn University, Linebacker (1981-84)*

TIGER WALK

When I was an Auburn football player, the Tiger Walk had not gained quite the popularity it has today, however it was pretty amazing. Let me try to explain in a few words what this magnificent walk meant to me in the early 1980's.

Competing on a collegiate level is a tremendous honor. Not only do you have the opportunity to do what you enjoy on the field, but it also provides the chance to perform in front of your classmates, peers, teachers, family, etc. In addition, you are offered the opportunity to earn one of the best educations in the country, in the halls of Auburn University.

Competing as an Auburn football player is an especially exciting undertaking. I had the opportunity to play in front of more than 72,000 fans in Jordan-Hare Stadium and today's player sees over 86,000 fans. But well before the aura of the fans inside the stadium at game time, is the Tiger Walk.

Each player has their own pre-game preparation, but when the time comes they get together as a team for the journey to Jordan-Hare Stadium. You can try to imagine but I don't know if there is a way to fully describe how you are feeling inside as you take that momentous walk to the stadium. You are focused on the game… of course… but you are definitely feeding off the emotion of the fans. It is almost hard to leave it behind and walk through the doors of the stadium. Your adrenaline is so high that you feel like you could run through a brick wall or pick up a car. This feeling carries you through pre-game warm-ups. As you return to the field from Coach Pat Dye's pre-game pep talk… you feel like you could explode as the wall of sound from the cheering fans hits you as you emerge from the tunnel.

I am speaking from a range of experiences in the NCAA and the NFL. I have played football in professional football stadiums all over the country, but there was nothing that compared to the intensity of the Tiger Walk, Jordan-Hare and the miraculous feeling the Auburn fans provide their team.

Auburn fans, always know that your voices are heard and your support is truly inspiring to the many athletes that have competed in the past and will compete in the future. You make a difference. For that, I thank you and now join in your cause.

It's Great to be an Auburn Tiger!

Dr. Gregg Carr
Birmingham, Alabama

Auburn University, Linebacker (1981-84)
Pittsburgh Steelers, Linebacker (1985-88)

"The Tailgating Rush"

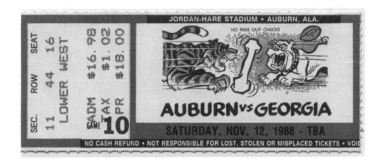

"Auburn vs. Georgia – November 12, 1988 - Ticket Stub"

"The crowd was growing ever larger and louder, so I just started forward and the band director jumped out of the way. I made it past the first intersection, but as I looked in my rearview mirror I was stunned by what I saw. It was like a scene from the movie "Braveheart" as the entire Georgia Band, lead by the geared-up band director, came charging over the hill by Cary Hall in a full gallop after us."

– Wayne Wiginton

AUBURN WINS – TROMBONE LOSES

Auburn vs. Georgia – November 12, 1988

I t was early November 1988. The Auburn Tigers, sporting an 8-1 record, were getting ready for their annual showdown with their cross-state rival Alabama (7-2) on Thanksgiving weekend. The only thing standing in the way was the Georgia Bulldogs (7-2), the team many still consider Auburn's biggest rival. I had decided to take my son, the pastor of our church and his wife down to the plains for this all-important game.

Little did I know that we would be in our own Auburn-Georgia showdown after the game. A showdown that would involve my van and a trombone.

It was your typical Auburn-Georgia game... right down to the wire. There was a lot riding on this game, since the winner would face the Florida State Seminoles (10-1) in the Sugar Bowl in New Orleans. The intensity on the field spilled over to the fans as Auburn pulled away in the final moments and ended up with a 20-10 win. We left the stadium in good spirits and headed back to our tailgating spot, totally unprepared for what was about to transpire.

We always parked in front of the Pharmacy Building and had never had any problems. However, on this particular Saturday, it appeared that some of the members of the Georgia Band were throwing a pity party. They were intentionally sitting and standing in the middle of the road, blocking traffic. One girl in particular, apparently distraught from the game's outcome, decided to sit directly in front of my van. I politely rolled the window down and asked her to move. But she didn't. After asking nicely, three or four times, I started inching towards her. When I was about one foot away from her, she reluctantly got up, stuck her head in my van window and began to curse violently. Had this been a male member of the band, I can assure you there would have been a physical confrontation. But I waited until she finished her tirade, removed her head from my vehicle, and then I proceeded to go on my way, extremely disturbed by her behavior.

As I pulled away, I heard an awful grinding metal sound. I looked back and the girl was yelling, "Stop! My trombone!" So I stopped, and by this time, the entire Georgia Band had gathered around my van. Then I heard someone say, "Let's turn his van over!" and they started hitting and kicking the van. I did not have a gun, but I told them I did in order to get them to stop. I believe the girl had been daring us to run over her instrument all along, but I hadn't noticed the trombone sitting in the road because I couldn't see over the nose of my van.

Their band director, still wearing his microphone and headgear, approached the van and stood in front, once again preventing me from going forward. I attempted to explain the situation, but the director either did not want to hear or could not hear because of his headgear. The crowd was growing ever larger and louder, so I just started forward and the band director jumped out of the way. I made it past the first inter-section, but as I looked in my rearview mirror I was stunned by what I saw. It was like a scene from the movie "Braveheart" as the entire Georgia Band, lead by the geared-up band director, came charging over the hill by Cary Hall in a full gallop after us. I could see the red and gray war paint on their faces, and the wood and metal weapons waiving in the air. I could hear the war drums beating as the overweight bass drummer was sprinting (in drum gear) towards us from the right flank of the charge. I quickly snapped back into action, frantically looking for an escape route. To my horror, there was nowhere to go.

I was actually getting a bit fearful, when I spotted the orange and blue cavalry at the next intersection. I was honking my distress horn to warn of the upcoming attack. Luckily, there were two police officers working the traffic. I called to one of them, and he walked over just as the angry crowd reached us. By this time there were literally hundreds of Auburn fans lining the street, waving their shakers in support. It turned out the police officer was with the campus police and could do nothing to resolve the situation. There was a brief standoff, which was resolved as the officer suggested that I trade contact information with one of Georgia's band officials.

A few weeks later, I received a very polite letter from the girl's father requesting that I pay for the trombone. I immediately picked up the phone and called him. He was shocked when I explained the situation, and even more disturbed when I told him that I had our pastor and his wife in the van with me. Needless to say, he refused my offer to pay for the instrument. It actually turns out that the girl was in need of a very quick replacement for her instrument because UGA was playing in the upcoming Gator Bowl against Michigan State.

BAD DOGGIE!!!

Wayne Wiginton
Jasper, Alabama

Tim and Laura Stanfield

"An Auburn man is someone who appreciates the railroad tracks you cross letting you know you're in Auburn. Someone who refers to Auburn as a village, rather than a city or town. Someone who will not tolerate the fan next to him booing at any AU player or coach. Someone who eats at Byron's Bar-B-Q while in Auburn. Someone who believes in the magic of a lucky hat, ticket stub, shirt or shaker."

– Tim Stanfield

THE AUBURN MAN

What is the "Auburn Man?" A child may say, "Someone who lives in Auburn." A scholar may say, "Someone who attended Auburn." A woman may say, "A well rounded guy yet, over-sure of himself." An Alabama fan may say, "Someone with more class than I understand."

But let me tell you what an Auburn man is to me.

An Auburn man is someone who feels the chill every time he passes Toomer's Corner. Someone who looks at Samford Hall and is in awe of it's greatness and beauty. Someone who appreciates a good, loud, away crowd. Someone who just likes to see the green of the grass inside Jordan-Hare Stadium.

An Auburn man is someone who appreciates the railroad tracks you cross letting you know you're in Auburn. Someone who refers to Auburn as a village, rather than a city or town. Someone who will not tolerate the fan next to him booing at any AU player or coach. Someone who eats at Byron's Bar-B-Q while in Auburn. Someone who believes in the magic of a lucky hat, ticket stub, shirt or shaker.

An Auburn man is someone who travels to an away game, even when we are not having the best season. Someone who has eaten at Country's Bar-B-Q for breakfast on game day. Someone who actually makes a point to stop by the Eagle's Cage on occasion. Someone who is not afraid to rattle off an old football story.

An Auburn man is someone that has celebrated at Toomer's after a big win. Someone that has seen an orange and blue sunset over the west side of the stadium. Someone that knows the story behind why we yell, "War Eagle." Someone who appreciates the specials at the Auburn Grill.

An Auburn man is also someone who stays to greet the players after a game when they laid it on the line. Someone who has been caught up in the moment and cried at a victory or defeat. Someone who has at least tried the "Mama's Love" at Mama Goldberg's. Someone who visits J&M Bookstore on game day.

An Auburn man has at least attempted to eat "The Pounder" at Cheeburger-Cheeburger. He's someone who arrives at the stadium an hour before a game. He's someone who can comprehend what Coach Pat Dye did for Auburn Football. He's someone who hated and still hates what happened to, "The Flush." He's also someone that can't sleep on Saturday mornings in the fall.

An Auburn man is someone like me.

Tim Stanfield
Birmingham, Alabama
AuburnUniversity
Class of 1999

'93

"Remember the Tigers"

1993 was a magical year for all Auburn fans. I don't think anyone dared to dream that this team would finish the season 11-0, whether they had been Auburn fans for a lifetime or just a few short weeks.

As a former Georgia fan, 1993 was significant for me, as well. My days as a Georgia fan were over, because it was also the year I came to Auburn.

I was raised a Georgia fan, and I had even attended Georgia for my first year of college, but I came to my senses in spring of 1993. I decided to transfer to Auburn.

The year I transferred to Auburn, Georgia was coming off one of its most successful seasons in a long time. The 1992 Georgia team won 10 games, including a victory over Ohio State in the Citrus Bowl. Garrison Hearst was runner up for the Heisman trophy, and Eric Zeier had once again put up huge passing numbers. Ray Goff appeared to have the Bulldogs poised for a successful run.

Auburn, on the other hand, was coming off one of its most disappointing seasons in years. The 1992 Tigers had a woeful record. The season ended with a loss to Alabama and Coach Pat Dye's resignation. With the 1993 season approaching, there was little reason for optimism on the Plains. Little did anyone know that over the next few years, the Auburn faithful would see more great football than many fans see in an entire lifetime.

The 1993 season started on a warm September night in Jordan-Hare Stadium. After an easy routing of Samford, the conference opener was a match up with Ole Miss. Auburn played well, and with the exception of a late kickoff return that made for a few tense moments, the Tigers beat the Rebels with relative ease. Two weeks later in Baton Rouge, Louisiana, Stan White would break Pat Sullivan's career passing record in a convincing road win at LSU.

Then the Tigers earned a hard-fought victory over Vanderbilt in Nashville, which was punctuated by a second-half goal-line stand. The Vandy game was sandwiched between home victories over Southern Miss and Mississippi State, and all three victories set the stage for a mid-October match-up with undefeated Florida. Even in light of the unbelievable 6-0 start, the mood on campus leading up to the showdown with the Gators could best be described as guarded optimism. An air of quiet confidence existed, but many believed this Auburn team had not yet been tested, and the Tigers were considered heavy underdogs to the mighty Gators.

When game day arrived, Jordan-Hare Stadium was packed with 85,000 of the most vocal college football fans I have ever heard. An hour before kickoff, more than half the stadium was full. I could hear boisterous cries of "War Eagle" from every direction. Although a light drizzle was falling, the gray skies overhead did nothing to dampen the spirits of this crowd.

By kickoff, there wasn't an empty seat in the house. Every time Danny Wuerffel stepped under center, a deafening roar arose from the stands. The crowd was determined to pull its team to a victory, regardless of what the odds makers or the media believed the outcome would be.

But early on, things did not go well for the Tigers. Florida jumped out to a quick 10-0 lead. Midway through the first quarter the Gators were again driving deep into Auburn territory. With Florida Coach Steve Spurrier's team seemingly assured of a third score, things looked bleak. Spirits were beginning to sink, and then something miraculous happened.

Midway through the first quarter, Wuerffel took a snap, made a short drop and fired a pass to his right. Calvin Jackson stepped in front of the intended receiver, intercepted the ball, and began running down the sideline. The crowd exploded. Calvin Jackson had blockers and a lot of running room. In a matter of seconds, he had streaked 90-plus yards and put six points on the scoreboard.

I'll never forget the way that play looked from my seat in the AU student section. At that moment, I think we genuinely believed that if we yelled loud enough we could somehow make Jackson reach the end zone faster. The emotional swing was incredible. Just when it looked like Florida was on its way to another easy win, that one play had changed the entire complexion of the game. Over the next few hours, we were treated to an incredible football game. The lead changed several times. There were other big plays, but none bigger than Jackson's interception.

When the contest was over, it could only be described as a classic. Both teams left everything on the field. Scott Ethridge's field goal with about a minute and a half left would end the scoring at 38-35. Sunday's Atlanta Journal-Constitution headline would proclaim, "Auburn in a Shocker."

On Saturday, November 13, 1993, I sat in Georgia's Sanford Stadium and helped cheer the Tigers to their 10th victory of the year. I had once bled red and black, but now I was pinning my hopes on the fortunes of the orange and blue. This was something I would have considered almost blasphemous just a few years earlier, but on that sunny November day in 1993, it seemed like second nature. It was an exciting ball game highlighted by Chris Shelling's interception return for a touchdown. We stayed and celebrated long after the final seconds had ticked away.

The mission this team had begun in early September was almost complete. The next Saturday, a victory over Alabama would be the culmination of an undefeated season, an outcome that no one could have possibly anticipated.

When I thought about writing a story for this book, my initial response was, "I've only been an Auburn fan since 1993." I didn't think my story belonged in a collection that was going to include the recollections of many life-long Tiger fans, especially considering that prior to 1993, I had been a dedicated Georgia fan.

My parents are both graduates of UGA, and I learned to cheer for the Bulldogs at a very young age. I can remember how excited my father became while listening to Larry Munson describe Hershel Walker's first college game. I also remember making trips with my family to Athens, Auburn, Starkville and Birmingham to watch the Bulldogs play.

I remember watching Sugar Bowl games against Notre Dame, Pittsburgh and Penn State on television in the early 1980s, Georgia's dominance of Florida in Jacksonville during Vince Dooley's tenure as coach, and yes, the infamous "fire hose" game at Auburn in 1986.

But I guess that's what makes my story so terrific. In 1993, Auburn had a magical season, and I had found not only a new team to cheer for, but a new home in Auburn, Alabama.

Jeffrey Mimbs
Birmingham, Alabama
Auburn University
Class of 1996

Sheri Catchings Thompson and Phillip Thompson

*"Coming off a losing season, on probation,
and just getting to know a new head coach,
no one had very high expectations for
this Tigers team, me included. But that
magical season truly began for me
with the best touchdown I never saw."*

— *Sheri Catchings Thompson*

THE BEST TOUCHDOWN
I NEVER SAW
"Auburn vs. Florida – October 16, 1993"

It was October 1993 - the fall quarter of my junior year. Coming off a losing season, on probation, and just getting to know a new head coach, no one had very high expectations for this Tigers team, me included. But that magical season truly began for me with the best touchdown I never saw.

The top-ranked Florida Gators were on the Plains that day, and even though my beloved Tigers had found ways to win the first few games, we were still a big underdog. The question didn't seem to be whether we'd lose the game that day, but how badly.

I wasn't able to make the start of the game since I had been stuck folding shirts at my job at J&M Bookstore. After the morning crowd came through to buy souvenirs, I made my way to the stadium just as I assumed the pre-game festivities would be concluding. I wasn't in too much of a rush, thinking I probably wouldn't miss much, even if I was a little late.

As I scurried past Foy Union and the stadium came into view, I heard a roar erupt from inside Jordan-Hare. "Oh no, surely Florida hasn't returned the kick-off for a touchdown," I thought in dismay. Then I realized I was now hearing the War Eagle fight song blasting through the stadium and that the cheering was WAY too loud for it to be coming from the visiting Gator fans.

"What the heck happened?" I thought, as I started to run... through the gate... up the ramp... and at last I met up with my friends. We had scored! Unbelievable! And what a momentum swing … Florida was already winning 10-0 and heading for another touchdown, when Auburn's Calvin Jackson intercepted Florida's Danny Wuerffel pass and returned it all the way to the end zone!

I may have missed Auburn's first touchdown, but there would be more to follow. And as every Auburn fan knows, not only did we beat the Gators that day, we beat everyone we played that season. And that awesome touchdown I never saw was just the first of many magical moments the Auburn faithful would experience that wonderful year.

Sheri Catchings Thompson
Birmingham, Alabama
Auburn University
Class of 1994

CRYING WITH STRANGERS

"Auburn vs. Alabama – December 2, 1972"

J ust about every Auburn fan you meet has a story about the Auburn-Alabama, 17-16, "Punt, Bama, Punt" game. My story not only reminds us of that amazing game, but of my parents' love for Auburn football.

We were at home watching the game on television. Halfway through the game, my mother had had enough. Her frustration and my father's repeatedly noisy tirades had driven her right out of the house and straight to the nearest shopping mall.

But unable to completely tear herself away from the action, Mom listened to the game on the radio as she drove to the mall. By the time she'd gotten to the mall and parked, Mom was so engrossed that she didn't even get out of the car, but sat and listened to the game. When Auburn blocked the second punt and took the lead, she began to scream and cry loudly. A gentleman had parked nearby and was walking by when he saw what he thought was a woman in real trouble. So he tapped on the window and asked what was wrong. When mother told him why she was crying, he started crying, too. He, obviously, was frustrated with the game's progress as well and had to get out of the house as well. So two complete strangers in Columbus, Georgia, shared a joyful, yet tearful, Auburn moment in a shopping mall parking lot.

Over the years as we've told and retold this story. We've always been proud and thankful that there are members of the Auburn family just about everywhere you go, and even more thankful that the stranger wasn't an Alabama fan.

Steve Kennedy
Fortson, Georgia

"Alan and Wayne Stanfield atop The Arc de Triumph - Paris, France"

"They were all also clad in some combination of orange and blue. But not the familiar burnt orange and rich navy blue of our beloved Auburn. These were the shocking neon shades of the Gators. We were right in the heart of enemy territory."

– Alan Stanfield

MY BEST ROAD TRIP EVER
"Auburn vs. Florida – October 15, 1994"

There are just some moments that are frozen in time, some athletes who do not age, and some games that are destined to be replayed over and over again in the memories of fans.

This is the story of one such game as remembered by a true fan, who witnessed it first-hand.

On Monday, I had no intention of making another long trip to "The Swamp," the place where I had been disappointed so many times before. But as Saturday grew closer, my brother, Wayne, called with an invitation to accompany him and his youngest son, Scott, on a last-minute trip to the game. And, being the committed Auburn fan that I am, I was almost obligated to my school and my team to go.

Who knew that what started as a spur-of-the moment trip would turn out to be a once-in-a-lifetime experience?

The first of what I like to call "omens" happened almost immediately as my brother started to back out of his driveway. A friend of Scott's, Bo Kerr, appeared out of nowhere with small-travel-bag-in-hand and ready to make the odyssey with us. He jumped in, made a quick call for a final thumbs-up from his family, and we were on our way.

The trip was fairly uneventful until about sunset. As we approached Dothan, I looked westward, and the second omen revealed itself. The sun was setting in an increasingly dark blue sky, and its beams produced a beautiful orange glow as it reflected from clouds on the horizon. An Auburn sunset. We were now ready to continue on our crusade of support, but also fully prepared to grin and bear the almost certain defeat to come. After all, we were 17-point underdogs.

As we neared Lake City, Florida, at about 1 a.m. and after many hours on the road, we decided we should get a little shut-eye. So we pulled into the only motel we could find with a vacancy sign. We soon found out why. But we were too tired to care, and after four to five hours of sleep and a hot shower, we were back on the road to Gainesville, but not before a stop at the local Waffle House for breakfast. The place was packed with Gator fans and cocky waitresses, but we held our own and left with a few parting shouts for the locals.

We hopped back into the van, and before we knew it, we started to notice college men in "wife-beater" shirts and nearly topless coeds, all tanned, in sunglasses, wearing slightly too short-shorts, and obviously in some stage of alcohol or drug-induced euphoria. They were all also clad in some combination of orange and blue. But not the familiar burnt orange and rich navy blue of our beloved Auburn. These were the shocking neon shades of the Gators. We were right in the heart of enemy territory.

Then, we witnessed another omen. With all of the traffic cruising down the main thoroughfare into Gainesville, who should pull up beside us at the next traffic light? It was another of Wayne's sons, Tim, with three of his buddies, Tommy, Mark and another Tim. The fickle finger of fate was pointing directly at us.

We soon found what we hoped was a safe parking spot and headed for the stadium. Our first objective... Tiger Walk.

As soon as we figured out that we were in the right place, our group set up shop at the exact exit point for the Auburn busses. We were some of the very first of the Tiger Walk supporters to arrive. After all, it didn't even begin for another hour.

We talked about the game, the season, past games and seasons, and told war stories of long ago road games. Then the crowd began to gather. At first, there were just a few. Then a few more. Soon there were near a hundred or so. And suddenly there he was... the Barney Fife of the University of Florida Campus Police Force. The rather short and stocky fellow approached and demanded to know what we thought we were doing. We explained the Tiger Walk tradition and attempted to put him at ease. But it was too late. He had a look of suspicion in his eyes as he informed us that we needed to stay back, even though we hadn't moved at all. The crowd had grown to the hundreds when he reached for his two-way radio and called for reinforcements. "I don't know what they're doin', but there's more and more of them comin'."

Soon, more campus police on bicycles began to arrive, and shortly thereafter, metal barriers and sawhorses were placed in front of the crowd, which had by now swelled to a thousand or more. An Auburn unicyclist and Aubie himself entertained the faithful. The Barney-from-Mayberry policeman apparently was convinced that the ever-growing crowd of Auburn supporters would suddenly turn into an uncontrollable horde that would trample the Florida fans on impulse, even though there were more policemen present than Gators.

Auburn videographers panned the now-frenzied crowd (the next day we saw ourselves on the coach's television show) and filmed the players, coaches and assorted other folk as they filed off the busses. There seemed to be a steely determination in the way the players navigated the Walk. There was a challenge ahead, but they seemed ready to meet it. The Tiger Walk crowd was in rare form. They yelled, sang and high-fived the players. It was the biggest away game Walk I'd ever seen. I started to think that maybe the best was yet to come.

We split up as the Tiger Walk ended, since our tickets were in different parts of the stadium. The tickets my brother and I ended up with turned out to be in the upper reaches of the southeast upper deck of Ben Hill Griffin Stadium. The others were scattered throughout the stadium, just as University of Florida officials had planned. They had dispersed the Auburn fans in order to dilute our impact on the game.

The final omen appeared just as we were settling into our seats. Climbing the stairs to the upper stratosphere seats, was a very, very, old Auburn fan, almost being carried by a burly security guard. His face was covered by an oxygen mask, and his wife pulled his oxygen tank up the numerous stairs. If this Old Tiger could pull a Lazarus act to watch us play, how could we lose?

Well, I'm sure you all are familiar with what happened on the field that day. A truly miraculous event unfolded before our eyes. But, to me, perhaps the best memories are of those peripheral events that surrounded our trip.

As the final seconds ticked down, I was overcome with a sense of wonder and amazement. I started to think I was having one of those out-of-body experiences. You know, the one where you're looking down at yourself from afar? And I literally had to shake myself back to reality.

But surprisingly, it was real. And, at the same time, it was slightly surreal. We had defeated the mighty Gators and

Coach Superior himself, and now we were cavorting with our own players, coaches and other fans outside the Auburn dressing room.

Although we had certainly discussed what type of gala celebration we would engage in that night, we were so thoroughly exhausted from our immediate post-game activities that we were unable to do much more than drink one final celebratory beverage and collapse into bed.

The next day, as we made our triumphant return, I knew I had completed my best road trip ever.

Alan Stanfield
Birmingham, Alabama
Auburn University
Class of 1963

AUBURN MEMORIES
LIVE ON

Life is filled with joy, but also with heartache. In my family, one way we deal with pain is by remembering the good times and continuing to carry on the traditions our lost loved ones held so dear... traditions like Auburn football. In fact, the memories our beloved Auburn Tigers have given my family over the years are some of my most cherished.

In 1963, I was 10 years old, and our family had moved to Tampa, Florida, from Birmingham, Alabama. We were in search of a warmer climate. My 38-year-old father was very ill with a kidney disease. I remember it like it was yesterday.

There was one area in Tampa where we were able to receive the faintest signal of WAPI radio, the pilot AM station for Auburn football that featured the great Buddy Rutledge. We would drive to this area of Tampa to listen to Auburn football in the car. Dad and the whole family enjoyed those times so much. In 1963, Auburn beat Alabama 10-8. It was such an exciting game, and it was the last game that my father heard before he died the following summer.

For years after, our family had 12 season tickets to Auburn games, thanks to my grandfather and namesake, Henry W. Sweet, who played at Auburn and is the reason we are an Auburn family. Tragically, my mother died suddenly in April 1972 at the young age of 44. On December 2, 1972, our entire family gathered at Legion Field for the Auburn-Alabama game. The only thing missing was our mother. Auburn was triumphant that day, beating Alabama 17-16. We celebrated that sweet victory in my mother's honor. We missed her desperately and wished she had been able to share in our celebration, but we also knew that she was somewhere smiling, knowing that her family was together and her Tigers were victorious.

In 1989, my grandfather, Henry W. Sweet, was the oldest living Auburn letterman. For him, his journey was finally complete when Alabama came to Auburn's Jordan-Hare Stadium that year and was defeated by the Auburn Tigers 30-20. He was 89 years old and in failing health, but he was in the stands. Coming into that game, Alabama was undefeated and ranked second in the nation. As the final seconds ticked off and my aunt helped my grandfather from the stadium, he and the rest of the family had tears in their eyes as we finally saw what many Auburn faithful had waited so many years to see. What a blessing it was for him! He passed away the following spring, but that game will go down as one of the most important games in Auburn football history and in my grandfather's life.

Thank you, Auburn, for the wonderful memories you've given my family. Your memories help ease the pain in life and celebrate the victories. War Eagle lives on forever!

Henry Sweet Breland
Tuscaloosa, Alabama
Auburn University
Class of 1977

Tracy Dowdy Hall, of the Auburn Alumni Association, with
Ed Burkhalter when the Rockdale/Newton Area Auburn Club
in Conyers, GA was presented their charter in 1997.

*"Well as the story goes, Ralph went to Athens
without a ticket or any possibility of getting one.
…After assessing the situation, Ralph picked up
some equipment the cheerleaders were bringing
into the stadium and walked right in! Yes, he
stood on the sidelines the entire game and was
never questioned about his credentials."*

– Edward H. Burkhalter, Jr.

SNEAKIN' THE DAWGS
"Auburn vs. Georgia – November 13, 1971"

Auburn played some of the greatest games in school history during 1971, but in my mind, no game was bigger than the 35-20 Auburn win over the Georgia Bulldogs.

I was a student at Auburn, it was an away game, and I simply could not find a ticket. I tried everything, including calling an old friend who was in his first year of law school at Georgia. He told me I was nuts to even call him. There were no tickets available, and he was leaving town that weekend. It seems Al was a recent industrial engineering graduate from Georgia Tech… now a law student… with little time for football.

Later that year, during my Christmas break/working holiday with an architecture firm, I was delighted to share a story about this game with my boss. His name was Gene, and he had also graduated from Auburn with a degree in architecture. Needless to say, Gene was a huge Auburn fan.

Gene shared his story about the fall of 1971 when he found himself sitting in the middle of the Georgia Alumni section during "the game." First, you need to know Gene's son, Buck, was attending Georgia at that time and constantly gave his father grief about Auburn. I am sure Gene was proudly sporting his Orange and Blue for the game, and I imagine he had a drink or two.

Gene told me that he was sitting quietly in the Georgia section during Auburn's first touchdown drive, and it nearly killed him. You would have to know Gene; he was not a quiet man. Well, when Auburn scored the second time, Gene could not contain himself any more; he stood up in the middle of the Georgia section and yelled "Warrrrrrrrrrrrrrrrrrrrrrrrrrrrrrrrrrrrrrrrrrrrrrrrr Damn Eagle!"

You would have to appreciate what Gene did that day. As most of us remember it was one of the most hostile football environments ever seen. He said from that moment on, there was no doubt that everyone on his side of Sanford Stadium knew who he was pulling for. It was definitely the guys in ORANGE and BLUE!

Of course you never want to top your new boss's story, but I had my Auburn-Georgia story to share, as well. As I mentioned earlier, I could not find a ticket to the game, but I had a roommate named Ralph, who was a lot more resourceful and determined.

Well as the story goes, Ralph went to Athens without a ticket or any possibility of getting one. As fate would have it, he was hanging around Sanford Stadium before the game and saw the cheerleaders arriving. After assessing the situation, Ralph picked up some equipment the cheerleaders were bringing into the stadium and walked right in! Yes, he stood on the sidelines the entire game and was never questioned about his credentials.

As the last seconds ticked off the clock, Ralph grabbed his piece of the legendary hedge and brought it back to Auburn, where it was proudly displayed in our apartment.

I do not remember whether Ralph's or Gene's story drew more attention from the listeners at the office, but it really does not matter. What does matter is that it's hard to beat sharing football stories with Auburn Fans everywhere.

Warrrrrrrrrrrrrrrrrrrrrrrrrrrrrrrrrrrrrrrrrrrrrrrrrrrrrrrrrrr Eagle!

Edward H. Burkhalter, Jr.
Conyers, Georgia
Auburn University
Class of 1973

"Auburn vs. USC Trip – Los Angeles, CA - September 2, 2002"
Mark, Tim, Wayne and Scott Stanfield

*"I have seen some great Auburn victories
in my time. But win or lose, I always know,
'It is Great to be an Auburn Tiger.'
I know that it's more than just a game…
it's a passion. And I thank my dad every
day for sharing that passion with me."*

– Tim Stanfield

WHAT AUBURN
MEANS TO ME

M y father had a very clear view about how he wanted to raise his sons. You need to know, up front, that this view was slightly tainted orange and blue, considering the fact that he graduated from Auburn in 1969, and there are no words that can sufficiently describe the depth of his commitment to his alma mater.

Consequently, he was bound and determined that his sons would grow up feeling the same way he did about Auburn.

Before we really got our hands around this whole Auburn thing, my brothers and I just thought he loved football and that was why he was such a ravenous Auburn fan. But we didn't mind it a bit. In fact, going to an Auburn football game with dad was one of the greatest joys a young Stanfield could experience. The night before, we would make all our preparations, which was very exciting in itself. As we packed, Dad would rattle off some old football story about how Auburn was a major underdog and ended up winning, thanks to some last-minute, awe-inspiring play. "Punt, Bama, Punt" was my personal favorite. He had the actual radio broadcast of that game on tape and used to play it for us on the way to games.

When game day arrived, we would usually head out before the sun came up. This really didn't bother me much, because I hadn't been able to sleep the night before anyway. On the way, we'd listen to some sports show on a fuzzy AM station. I always loved it when we could pick up the "Leonard's Loser's" show, even though dad had warned me that Leonard was partial to Georgia.

We would drive through Hardee's to get breakfast and eat it on the road, so we didn't lose any time. I loved the car rides to Auburn with my dad, older brother, occasionally my uncle and later my younger brother. The entire way, we talked of nothing but sports. Girlfriends, school, grades and work were never mentioned. Those were the best conversations in the world.

Even as a youngster, I knew that when we turned off Highway 280 at the Conoco station, we were getting close. I loved seeing the fisheries and going over the railroad tracks into the heart of Auburn. The town would be buzzing with excitement; people were everywhere, all yelling out "War Eagle" without hesitation. How cool is that to a kid? "WAR EAGLE!"

We would park, throw the football around for a while and then it was off to J & M Bookstore to get our face painted, get a shirt or some Auburn souvenir that we would take to school the next Monday for "show and tell." If we had time, we would go by Toomer's drugstore for some lemonade. And once in the game, we'd all pitched in a dollar of our own money to get a group program.

All those things my father showed me, taught me, and told me about Auburn had a dramatic impact on me. I always knew I would go to Auburn, and I graduated from "The Loveliest Village on the Plains" in 1999. I have seen some great Auburn victories in my time. But win or lose, I always know, "It is Great to be an Auburn Tiger."

I know that it's more than just a game … it's a passion. And I thank my dad every day for sharing that passion with me.

Tim Stanfield
Birmingham, Alabama
Auburn University
Class of 1999

FROM THE BLEACHERS:
AUBURN WINS
WITH CLASS

"Auburn vs. Georgia – November 18, 1978"

As a former player and a genuine admirer of Auburn and everything it stands for, I am compelled to share this experience, "From the Bleachers," with you.

One November afternoon, after my playing days were over, I was sitting in the south end zone of Jordan-Hare Stadium and was fortunate enough to strike up a conversation with the mother of one of the Auburn players. Her son was playing for the Tigers against Georgia, and we shared pleasantries as we prepared for the game to begin.

Suddenly, some acquaintances of mine from Sylvester, Georgia, adorned in their best Red and Black, showed up to claim their seats. They were rowdily cheering for their team, and it was obvious that they had consumed some alcohol. As they began to settle into their seats behind me, I spoke to them and tried to be gracious. They whooped and hollered and barked in my face. I continued to try my best to ignore these antics, but could see the alcohol was taking control.

As the game progressed, the Georgia fans became even more unruly. The nice lady and I had just about had enough of their language and their behavior. I was on the verge of expressing discontent when I heard the sound of alcohol pouring out of a bottle, but then missing its mark and spilling out onto the floor. They cussed each other as the "Wild Turkey" splashed its way down the steps. As I said, I was on the verge of expressing my displeasure with their actions when the player's mother boldly said, "If you were a 'TRUE DAWG,' you would get down there and lick that up." This lady was a very nice lady of large stature, and I imagine that most of the time, when she speaks to people, they listen to her.

Needless to say, the Dawg fans were quiet for the rest of the game. And the lady and I had a good laugh at their expense. Truth is, I cannot remember the outcome of the game, but Auburn won with CLASS in the stands that day.

As I have traveled with the Tigers across the country, I've had many more of these types of experiences. I was at LSU for the erroneously "blown whistle call." I was at Jordan-Hare Stadium for the fire. I was at Sanford Stadium when we won while they had Hershel Walker. I was at the Swamp when we drained it. I love Auburn football, but I am equally proud of the Auburn traditions and the class of the Auburn people. They really are what make Auburn such a great place!

Bubba Ivey
Albany, Georgia
Auburn University
Class of 1978

Jesse Jones and his grandmother, Juanita Jones

"It's more than just football, more than sports.
Period. It's a state of mind, a feeling, a way of life.
Right there under God, family, and country, is
Auburn. I love it, I support it and I defend it."

– Jesse Jones

SOME JUST
DON'T GET IT
"Real Auburn Tigers Cry Joyful Tears"

I am a 23-year-old male, so technically, I'm not supposed to cry. Particularly, not in public. But I'll be honest: I have openly cried tears of joy while watching our Auburn Tigers win.

I remember crying more than once during the 1993 season. It was a special year for me. I had always gone to Auburn games growing up, but I'd never made it to every game in a season, including road games. Not until 1993.

It was never really our intention, but somehow my grandparents, my father and I were able to make every game in 1993, from the early-season, Saturday-night showdown in Death Valley, to that homemade miracle at Auburn against the mighty Florida Gators. Then on to frozen Fayetteville, and eventually wrapping up a perfect season in Auburn against the despised Crimson Tide. It was, indeed, perfect, and well worth swallowing a little of my manly pride to shed a few tears.

I did a little crying on the road during the 1993 LSU game and the 2000 Georgia game. I had been able to make a couple of road games in 1992, but we had lost both times. (Ole Miss 45-21, and Mississippi State 14-7) I was determined that I would watch my Tigers be victorious on the road. And in 1993, I got my chance. I'll never forget standing with my father on the walkway around the field at Death Valley. I was 15 years old, and we were giving the team "high-fives" as they came off the field and into the locker room after romping LSU 34-10. I looked at the players' faces and then looked at my father. We were all smiles (and a few tears). It felt so great to be an AUBURN TIGER that night.

I remember watching Auburn versus Georgia in 1992, feeling helpless as the last few seconds ticked off the clock and we lost 14-10. I was devastated (but didn't cry then, however). Then, in 1994, we had to watch our winning streak end at 20 games as a two-touchdown lead evaporated in the fourth quarter. At the time, a 23-23 tie felt as bad as a loss. And, of course, everyone remembers the 1996 game with the four overtimes in Auburn. And, in 1998, well, we were simply a down team and overpowered in 28-17 defeat in Auburn. Loving Auburn the way I do, I hated losing to Georgia at home so many years in a row, and it stung even more losing the way we did.

So, in 2000, there we were, knocking on the door of the SEC West Championship, and the only thing that stood in our way was Georgia. The game was everything I expected it to be, and then some. It was an emotional roller coaster that still wasn't decided after regulation. For as long as I live, I will never, ever, forget big number 32 (Rudi Johnson) rumbling down to the one yard line in overtime to set up Ben Leard's one-yard sneak into the end zone for the win. I hugged my grandmother, and we hollered, cried, screamed and cried some more. We had finally done it. We had finally beaten Georgia again at our place, and in what fashion. Wow! Don't you just love Auburn? (A quick side note: The 2001 win over Georgia was sweet revenge for the game Auburn lost to Georgia in 1992. You may remember in 2001, Georgia fans, at home in Athens, watched as the last few seconds ticked off the clock in their loss to Auburn.)

In case you can't tell, I'm pretty hooked on Auburn. To me, there will never be an athlete as gifted as a Bo Jackson, and there will never be anything as great as being an Auburn fan. If you understand, your eyes are almost brimming with tears of pride right now as you read this. You can't really explain it; you either "get it," or you don't. That's just it. Auburn is everything that feels good and right in the world. And Alabama fans will never get that. It's more than just football, more than sports. Period. It's a state of mind, a feeling, a way of life. Right there under God, family, and country, is Auburn. I love it, I support it and I defend it.

I have never had the opportunity to attend school at Auburn. But I will one day… it's my dream. There are those who wonder how I could love Auburn so much if I've never gone to school there or even lived there. But they are the ones who will never really understand Auburn, where it came from, and how far it has come… particularly not folks from the "other" school.

You see, we'll always be huge rivals with the University of Alabama because, in their eyes, we'll always be beneath them. They think of us as that little "cow college." They will never really understand Auburn, and in many ways they will never be able to have what we have down in Auburn – family, a tight-knit family from so many different walks of life that are able to come together and share a common sense of pride.

And I mean pride. If you're like most folks in this country, you are proud when you say you are an American. I experience that same pride when I say that I am a United States Marine. And I feel the same strong emotions every time I think of Auburn, and every time I shout, "It's great to be an Auburn Tiger!" I feel it when I pass a fellow fan on the sidewalk and exchange "War Eagles." And, yes, even when I cry those tears of joy.

That sense of pride almost overwhelms you when you're actually in Jordan-Hare Stadium on a clear game day, when the sun is setting and the sky is turning a beautiful orange and blue. At that moment, if you take a second to look at the sea of orange and blue around you, then look at the sunset, you know you are home. And you know that as long as that sun rises and sets, there will be an Auburn.

You also know that wherever you go, Auburn will always go with you. It lives eternally in the hearts and minds of all those who love Auburn. There's no place like it, anywhere. If you're still reading, I know you probably feel the same way.

My grandparents went to Auburn back in the early 1940s. My grandmother still loves to tell me how she went to Auburn when it was still API (Alabama Polytechnic Institute). And they've been die-hard Auburn fans ever since. Throughout my life my grandparents have told me, particularly when things weren't going just right down on the Plains, "Jesse, just love Auburn, and the rest will take care of itself." That's exactly what I do. And always will.

War Eagle Everyone!

Jesse Jones
Birmingham, Alabama

Toomer's Corner

"The True Measure of an Auburn Man is His Children"
L-R: Neal, Valery, Chris and his wife Chanel

"During that amazing game,
Sherrie experienced a true conversion.
She was so impressed with the 'never-say-die'
attitude of the Auburn fans that she got
caught up in the excitement.
…On the way back to Auburn after the
game, I proposed, and Sherrie accepted."

– Richard Cotton

WHAT GOD (AND AUBURN) HAVE GIVEN ME

I came from very meager means… the backwoods of South Alabama, to be exact. But I owe everything I have today to God, who I believed played a great part in sending me to Auburn University. Today I enjoy a successful career with a great company, which was made possible with a scholarship to Auburn and the Chemical Engineering degree I received there in 1974.

But that is really just the beginning of my Auburn story. Truth is, I also give Auburn credit for the fact that my wife, Sherrie, and I have been happily married for 30 years.

You see, my wife was a lifelong Alabama fan until she went with my roommate, his fiancée and me to the 1972 Auburn-Alabama game (the miracle, "Punt-Bama-Punt" game). During that amazing game, Sherrie experienced a true conversion. She was so impressed with the "never-say-die" attitude of the Auburn fans that she got caught up in the excitement. Her change of heart was already underway long before Coach Ralph "Shug" Jordan sent in our field goal team to make the score 16-3. On the way back to Auburn after the game, I proposed, and Sherrie accepted.

Our lifelong relationship with Auburn continues through the years. In fact, our oldest son, Chris, and the son of my roommate (with whom we went to the 1972 game) were also roommates at Auburn from 1995-1999 and football managers for Coaches Terry Bowden, Bill Oliver and Tommy Tuberville. Chris graduated from Auburn in 2000, married a beautiful young lady (also an Auburn graduate) in 2002, and they are happily settled now in Birmingham, Alabama.

And to this day, more than 30 years later, our entire family remains Dye-hard Auburn fans who will be forever grateful for everything Auburn University has given us over the years.

Richard Cotton
Baker, Louisiana
Auburn University
Class of 1974

Mark and Elise Stanfield

Basil Bohannon

"To this day it remains the only Auburn - Alabama game played on foreign soil that I've ever heard of. The field was lined with tanks, and they had air support just in case they got caught off guard. …And, just like all the other Auburn - Alabama games in history, it turned out to be a good one."

– Bo Bohannon

AUBURN VS. ALABAMA 1944:
"A War Within A War, But One With No Losers"

I t was the fall of 1944. The Allied troops were fighting their way through France and Belgium, moving painstakingly toward the Battle of the Bulge, which would prove to be the final German offensive and the end of World War II.

A student at Auburn University when he enlisted in June of 1942, my father, Basil Bohannon, was one of those brave soldiers … a member of the 82nd Airborne … who in the fall of 1944 was somewhere in France risking everything to help bring an end to that terrible conflict.

My father was playing baseball at the time he enlisted, as he was a letterman in three sports, and also training for the football season. One of his friends stated, "Bohannon still had his baseball uniform on when he enlisted." And like virtually all of his fellow soldiers, whenever there was a break in the action, his thoughts always turned to home.

In fact, whenever they had the chance, the soldiers would quickly hustle up a game of baseball or football, not only to remind them of home, but also to help alleviate the tension. They mostly played those two sports because you really didn't need much equipment. Remember, it wasn't like they had a footlocker filled with balls and bats and pads and helmets. They just made do with what they could find.

But that was okay. They loved to play. And even sometimes they'd get in trouble for letting the games go too long and not paying enough attention to the business at hand.

It happened that during the Fall of 1944, the 82nd airborne unit got wind that the Rose Bowl was about to be played back home. So they decided they'd have a bowl game of their own. They'd have their own Iron Bowl, right there in France. Surprisingly enough, some of the members of the unit had actually attended either Auburn or Alabama, or at least were fans. The rest just had to pick a side.

Like I said before, there was no equipment. There wasn't even a ball. But they made do, and a rugby ball they managed to scrape up worked just fine. Sure they had helmets, but the ones they wore to fight were too heavy and moved around on their heads too much. Plus, a couple of officers who knew about the game told them that if anyone got hurt, they couldn't come to the medical tent. It wasn't for football injuries, and they couldn't spare the supplies. But that didn't discourage the players a bit. And they pressed on with their game-day preparations.

To this day it remains the only Auburn - Alabama game played on foreign soil that I've ever heard of. The field was lined with tanks, and they had air support just in case they got caught off guard. There were two full regimens … around 1,500 to 2,000 people … on hand to watch. And, just like all the other Auburn - Alabama games in history, it turned out to be a good one.

You'll be glad to know that as the game clock was winding down, the Auburn team had the lead. But then the men just started substituting in on both sides. Because, you see, it wasn't about a score that day. It wasn't about who beat whom.

It was about taking some time away from the fear. It was about coming together and forgetting about reality for a while. But even more importantly, it was about remembering the things you love and cherish about home. It was about remembering and honoring the great things about being American and being free.

Bo Bohannon
Birmingham, Alabama

"Capital One Bowl – Auburn vs. Penn State - Orlando, FL – January 1, 2003"
Back Row: John Lilac, Mark Vines, Tim Stanfield, David Ferrell and Jeff Mimbs
Front Row: Scott Stanfield, Wayne Stanfield and Pete Kanakis

"I think about some of the Auburn football clichés
around like "Punt, Bama, Punt," "The Kick,"
"The Reverse" and "Bo Over the Top."
I would throw "Defense, Auburn, Defense"
right in the mix."

– Mark Vines

FAVORITE GAMES
I ATTENDED

Auburn-LSU – September 20, 1997 – This was known as the Dameyune Craig versus Cecil "The Diesel" Collins game… a battle of two amazing athletes. They both drove their teams up and down the field. Dameyune put a drive together in the fourth quarter that was simply amazing, winning the game for us. I really don't remember everything about the game except how well those two played, and that Auburn won, 31-28. Any opposing fan who has been to "Death Valley" knows how hard it is to go in there and to pull off a victory. I really can't describe what it was like for us to win that game, but no one expected us to prevail, or to play in the SEC championship.

Auburn-Alabama – November 20, 1993 – I'd gone to my share of Auburn-Alabama games, but for some reason, I'd never seen us win one. This one was different, however. 1993 was the 11 and 0 season. The game was in Auburn. What I remember most was James Bostic's 70-something yard touchdown in the fourth quarter, which basically put the lid on the game. He just took off and ran, and he wasn't touched until he was in the end zone. After he scored, he was celebrating and looking to the student section, when Tony Richardson, our full back, put the hardest hit I have ever seen on him. It was certainly the hardest hit James had taken all day. Tony already had his helmet off and they just went head to head, crashing into each other as the place went insane. Of course, it's always great to beat Alabama, but to beat them and go undefeated that season was amazing.

Another little thing I remember was that Mike Ditka was doing the NFL broadcast on the Sunday after Florida State had won the national championship. He and the other commentators were talking about how FSU Coach Bobby Bowden finally got his championship, and Ditka just said, "Yeah a Bowden deserved the national championship, but they gave it to the wrong Bowden. Terry should have gotten it because they were they only ones that went undefeated."

Of course we couldn't go to a bowl that year, but... 11 and 0 is as good as it gets! In my mind we were the national champions. I know we didn't get the recognition or a trophy but what is a national championship... really? It is winning every game that you play, and that's what we did.

Auburn-LSU – September 17, 1994 – This one is simply known as "Defense, Auburn, Defense." We still had the winning streak going, but that team didn't play well offensively. Chris Shelling, Auburn's free safety and my favorite defensive player of all time, had a great game with two interceptions and a fumble recovery for a touchdown. Shelling's fumble recovery was early in the game, but after that, LSU was beating us up and down the field. They were kicking field goals and throwing touchdowns. The coaches pulled Nix and put in Dameyune. He didn't do any better. The offense just couldn't get it going. Miraculously, we scored three defensive touchdowns in the fourth quarter, all of them interceptions returned for touchdowns. For some reason, they kept throwing the ball, and we kept intercepting it. The first one was by Ken Alvis, who intercepted a pass and ran it back for a touchdown. Then Fred Smith got his pick and touchdown, and the third one by Brian Robinson. At the end of the game, I was exhausted. I had sweated and cheered and yelled so much that my friends and I just sat in the stadium for 30 minutes after the game ended. We were so drained, we couldn't move. We had gone through so many different emotions… I doubt I will ever see anything like that again. We really didn't deserve to win that game, based on the way our offense played, but our defense sure deserved the victory. Our defense outscored their entire team. I think about the well known Auburn football clichés like "Punt, Bama, Punt," "The Kick," "The Reverse" and "Bo Over the Top." I would throw "Defense, Auburn, Defense" right in the mix. It wasn't an Alabama game… and nothing means as much as those… but to me it's one of those magical moments. You can walk up to any Auburn fan and say, "Defense, Auburn, Defense," and everyone knows exactly what game you are talking about. Certainly Auburn folks would have to rank this as one of the best.

Auburn-Florida – October 16, 1993 – No one gave us a chance… especially me. Florida came to Auburn ranked number one in the nation. They marched out of the locker room and started whipping us. It was 10-0 early in the game, and they were about to score again. You could just feel the negative energy in the stadium. They were about to put the dagger in us. I think everybody thought, "Well here they go, they're going to run up the score." And then Calvin Jackson happened. He intercepted the ball, and it seemed like it took him three days to run down the field to score that touchdown. We have already talked about going from one extreme emotion to the other during a game, but nothing was as strong as that moment. We were instantly back in the game. We really thought it was going to be 17-0 and instead it was a three-point game.

I was with 10 of my friends in the student section on the first row of the upper section on about the 20-yard line. In the time it took Calvin to run the interception back, I had somehow made it from one side of our group to the end. I remember jumping on top of one of my friends, nearly killing him. We were all jumping up and down, going insane. Of all the times I've been in Jordan-Hare Stadium, that was the loudest I can remember. When he got that touchdown we knew ... we knew that somehow we were going to win that game. And we did. We fought the entire game, and then Scott Etheridge kicked the game-winning field goal.

Auburn-Florida – October 15, 1994 – "The Swamp" in Gainesville, Florida, was the site of the best college football game I have ever seen. It was up and down the field, offense and defense. It had everything. There was Pat Nix, an average quarterback, but he would have won the Heisman Trophy, if it were based on that game. Andy Fuller, who had hardly caught a pass all season, caught pass after pass and was an instant All-American tight end. Frank Sanders made some amazing plays, such as the reverse he ran for a touchdown and the final catch, just to name a few. Thomas Bailey had a touchdown at the beginning of the game. Willie Gosha, who was number 32 at the time, had a fourth-down catch and miraculously dragged his toe to stay in bounds. It was one of the best clutch catches I've ever seen. What many people never saw (I know I have never seen any footage of it) was when Frank Sanders caught the game-winning touchdown, Tyrone Goodson, who was on the other side of the field, came running across the end zone and did a front flip in the air.

The defense was outstanding, shutting down Terry Dean, Florida's quarterback and a Heisman Trophy candidate. Truth is, that game essentially ended his career. He got yanked, and they put in this unknown quarterback named Danny Wuerful. Both teams had played very well. It just came down to who had the ball last. And fortunately, we had the ball last!

Mark Vines
Birmingham, Alabama
Auburn University
Class of 1997

THE DISTRACTING
ROAR OF VICTORY

"Auburn vs. Florida – October 15, 1994"

I t was a warm Saturday in the autumn of 1994. I was first chair of the flute section in our high school band and was marching in Troy State University's homecoming parade, the last parade I would march in before my graduation. I heard the roar of victory that day.

Although I was excited about being in the parade, it wasn't my first choice of places to be that day. Auburn University (AU), the college I would be attending in less than a year, was taking on the Florida Gators in "The Swamp." And I wanted to be camped out on my parent's couch watching the game.

As participants in the parade, we had complimentary tickets to Troy's game, which was coinciding with Auburn's rumble with Florida. At the game, everyone was huddled in little groups, usually around one person with a Walkman. We waited anxiously as Auburn continued to hold its own with Florida, never more than three points ahead or three points behind.

As the day grew darker and as the Troy State stadium became colder, the Auburn-Florida game dwindled into its last couple of minutes. AU's Frank Sanders made an amazing catch for one last touchdown, and we counted down the last 10 seconds. The breath we had all been simultaneously holding came out in one deafening "ROAR" as more than three-fourths of the people in the stadium rose in celebration.

The campus police had to go around "shushing" everyone. It turns out that Troy State had been in the middle of calling a play when the Auburn game had ended. All the screaming had distracted the players, who were looking up to see what was going on. They were probably the only ones who had no idea what just happened. Auburn had just won a pivotal game and became only the second team in history to beat a Steve Spurrier coached Florida team at home in "The Swamp."

I remember that moment… and that roar of victory… like it was yesterday.

War Damn Eagle!

Leslie Carpenter Murphy
Birmingham, Alabama
Auburn University
Class of 1999

Barbara and Alan Stanfield

*"…and it was Alan who made the young
nephew riding on his shoulders wait five
minutes to go to the bathroom until Auburn
scored against Florida. And it was also
Alan who paid a wet price for that decision."*

– Barbara Hewitt Stanfield

AN AUBURN MARRIAGE

"Auburn vs. Georgia Tech – October 19, 1963"

"**Y**ou have 15 minutes to decide," Alan said, impatiently. "Do you want to go back to Jobe Rose, Service Merchandise or Bromberg's?"

It was 1963 and the day we were picking out my engagement ring. I was literally being pulled through the streets of downtown Birmingham. You see, I had seen rings at three stores and was being urged to make up my mind, and fast. No, the stores weren't about to close. And there wasn't a nasty storm coming. It was 15 minutes before the kickoff of the 1963 Auburn versus Georgia Tech game. The game was about to come on the radio. So we ran, hand in hand, up the street, to the parking lot, just in time to tune in.

I remember that day like it was yesterday. It was the day I got engaged. But what I don't remember is who won the game. But one thing's for sure, Alan does. He can tell you all the details of that 29-21 game, and any other game, for that matter.

To be honest, I've never asked him why he didn't pick out my ring and plan some romantic moment to present it to me. Some girls find their ring at the bottom of a glass of wine; some are escorted to the site of their first date and presented with the all-important token of everlasting love. My own daughter found her ring on our Christmas tree where her precious John had carefully placed it inside a Christmas decoration.

But not me. You would think that day in 1963 would have been a clear sign. I should have seen the handwriting on the wall from the very beginning. It just took me a while to realize how important Auburn would be in my life, my whole life.

For example, we had originally planned a honeymoon to a then non-commercialized Gatlinburg, because I love the mountains and the romantic atmosphere there. You see, our wedding was to take place on December 28, 1963, and I dreamed of snow-covered mountains and a cozy cottage in which to snuggle up for our honeymoon.

Now here's a test for all you Dye-hard Auburn fans: do you remember anything significant about 1963? That's right... Auburn got a bid to the Orange Bowl! And, as you can imagine, my honeymoon plans changed. In the middle of the Union Building in Auburn, Alan tenderly asked, "Would you mind if we went to Miami instead of Gatlinburg? Auburn is going to play Nebraska in the Orange Bowl, and this is a chance of a lifetime."

And, being a totally codependent person eager to please my love at all cost, I agreed. The plans were changed, and we headed south. Now, I love the snow, and we rarely get it in Birmingham. But on the weekend we left for Miami, Birmingham got a record snowfall and so did Gatlinburg. Oh, what we do for love!

Once again, I don't remember much about that game, either. But I do remember looking at the field, seeing how BIG the Nebraska players were and just praying we didn't get killed. That would really put a damper on my honeymoon. The good news is, we did okay, 7-13, even if we didn't win. By the way, Alan can give you the play-by-play of that game, too, if you're interested.

So I guess it's an understatement to say that Auburn has infiltrated every aspect of our marriage and family life since our engagement. Now, don't get me wrong, I dearly love Auburn. And I quickly defend her to anyone who even looks like they have something negative to say. Every fall you can find me at most games cheering wildly for Auburn and reprimanding any Auburn fan casting aspersions on our team.

But for Alan, now that's a whole different story. Alan is the one who had our children refusing to walk under a red umbrella when a kindergarten teacher wanted to escort them to our car in the driving rain; it was Alan who dragged our family of four to all home games; and it was Alan who made the young nephew riding on his shoulders wait five minutes to go to the bathroom until Auburn scored against Florida. And it was also Alan who paid a wet price for that decision.

Although I may poke fun and tell tales, I'm proud that Auburn has been a significant part of my life since the early 1960s. I'm proud of the fact that the Auburn spirit is so powerful that it really cannot be defined. And I am so thankful that it is an integral part of my marriage, my soul and my character. May God bless America, Auburn and Auburn fans everywhere.

War Eagle!

Barbara Hewitt Stanfield
Birmingham, Alabama
Auburn University
Class of 1965

Langdon Hall – Auburn University
Photo submitted by Cathy Henry

*"Words can't really describe it. It's
impossible to explain the emotion
you experience when you take that
deep breath, feel the temperature drop
and know the 'season of seasons' is here."*

– Illia Ayers

THE BREEZE

It's tough to explain, but I believe there's something sacred... almost supernatural... about Auburn. I remember almost feeling giddy when I walked to class each day during my years on the Plains. It just seemed like the rich tradition, the majestic architecture and the beautiful girls all blended into a perfect wonderland, and I was lucky to be a part of it.

But as wonderful as it was the rest of the year, there was something in the fall air at Auburn that was really magical.

Perhaps you need to experience it for yourself to really understand it, but there seemed like there was always one miraculous moment each fall in Auburn for me. It would typically happen in the early evening while I was walking home from class. It was a moment that made me feel invigorated and invincible. As the changing leaves rustled in the breeze, I knew I had just experienced the magic: I had just inhaled the first cool breeze of an Auburn autumn.

That breeze is still as enchanting for me today as it was years ago, because it still means the same thing today... football season has arrived. You've probably smelled it in the air and felt it in your heart. Words can't really describe it. It's impossible to explain the emotion you experience when you take that deep breath, feel the temperature drop and know the "season of seasons" is here. It's a giddy, childlike feeling all over again, which is sort of tough to explain to a wife or girlfriend who doesn't understand. (But don't get me wrong; that's not to say that there aren't women who feel it, too.)

I wonder? Is it the combination of the cool air and anticipation that brings football season to life? Does this raw excitement we have stored deep in our brains release strange endorphins when we inhale that first breeze? It probably doesn't happen to everyone. And it might just happen to a few of us... those Auburn fans who truly love the game and their team. But I don't think this experience is so rare after all. I personally know quite a few others who have also claimed to have experienced what I call "the breeze."

If you never experienced the sensation of the breeze, maybe you never will. For those of you who have, you probably always will. For those of you who are waiting for it, it may come to you, and I hope it does, because there's nothing quite like it.

Illia Ayers
Birmingham, Alabama
AuburnUniversity
Class of 1997

"Auburn at the South Pole – October 29, 2001"

Meghan Prentiss is a 25-year-old Brown University graduate from
Norwell, Massachusetts and niece of Paul W. Heaton, Auburn Class
of 1961 and cousin of Paul W. Heaton Jr., Auburn Class of 1982.
At the time Meghan was a weather researcher at South Pole for
Raytheon. Knowing the significance of AU in the life of her relatives,
she took an AU flag and flew it there and took these photos.
Photo submitted by Charles Heaton of Birmingham, Alabama.

Tiger, Dowe Aughtman and daughter, Catherine

"Our family is grateful to Auburn for our memorable years, experiences and for our educations. Our Auburn educations have enabled us to succeed in life and contribute to our country. Auburn has been a second home to us since the 1940s; it is truly a part of our family lineage."

— Mary Claire (Aughtman) Janiga

WAR EAGLE LINEAGE

I graduated from Auburn in 1971, just as I had known since childhood that I would. You see, I was brought up in an Auburn family, and tales of gridiron glory and college life on the plains were constants in my house.

My uncles Monk and Frederick Gafford played football for Auburn in the 1940s. Uncle Monk still held records for the Auburn-Georgia game when I was in school in the 1960s. I remember my grandmother telling us tales about letters she had received during World War II from soldiers who had watched an Auburn exhibition game, during which General Patton got so excited that he fell out of the stands while watching my Uncle Monk run for a touchdown. Uncle Monk lived to celebrate his induction into the Auburn Hall of Fame.

My oldest cousin attended Auburn and dated football star Vince Dooley, who was later head football coach at the University of Georgia. While I was in Auburn, I worked part-time for Fob James, another Auburn record holder and an Alabama governor. A year after I started school, my sister joined me at Auburn, along with five cousins. Those years were wonderful. Auburn was truly a family school, and we all thrived in varying sororities, fraternities and schools of study. But, little did we know how much we were influencing our younger brother, Dowe, who watched us come and go on the weekends.

My sister and I were teenagers when our younger brother Dowe Aughtman came along. We were thrilled to have a boy in the family, and our parents were overjoyed. Our parents were older when Dowe was born, and we all worried that he might be a sissy. But our little brother began to prove his athletic prowess by winning the local Punt, Pass and Kick competitions and playing football, baseball and golf. We were all ecstatic when he signed to play at Auburn. Our parents were so proud and had so many wonderful years at Auburn watching him play. We still laugh today about thinking he might be a sissy!

Dowe went on to play professional football with the Dallas Cowboys, but today he lives in Auburn with his wife, Brenda, another Auburn graduate whose parents are such Auburn devotees that they donated the Auburn female athletic dorm. Dowe and Brenda have two daughters who will undoubtedly continue the Auburn lineage.

Our family is grateful to Auburn for our memorable years, experiences and for our educations. Our Auburn educations have enabled us to succeed in life and contribute to our country. Auburn has been a second home to us since the 1940s; it is truly a part of our family lineage. We are proud to be Auburn alumni and our motto will always be WAR EAGLE!

Mary Claire (Aughtman) Janiga
Midlothian, Virginia
Auburn University
Class of 1971

CONVERTING FROM CRIMSON

A long, long time ago, 1938 to be exact, my father's father graduated from the University of Alabama. He met my grandmother who had lived in Tuscaloosa all of her life while he was at college. She never went to college, but my grandmother had eight siblings who all lived in Tuscaloosa. Actually they still do along with their offspring, and their offspring's offspring, and their offspring's...you get the picture. Then of course, following in my granddad's footsteps, my father attended Alabama. He met my mom and they both graduated in 1965.

Every year we had family reunions at my great aunt's compound. I say compound, because it was more like a development of family residents plopped on a piece of land with a pond in the middle and a social gathering place conveniently located by the pond. These reunions were enormous, but the funny thing is that most of the family already lived within a few miles of one another. The family reunions were apparently for the families like mine who had flown the coup for one reason or another and moved away. Still, to this day, these family members of mine gather together every second Sunday in May. At these gatherings every dirty football joke is told and retold, and all of Alabama's victories are told and retold. Football trash talk amongst the adults takes over. And I could never leave "The Bear" stories out. My granddad actually was a student at Alabama while "The Bear" was a football player. A lot of these people/fans are graduates, but all of them are season ticket holders. In addition, like many fanatical fans, they forbid any outsiders to marry into the family nor would they allow their offspring to attend the rival teams school.

I grew up in Knoxville, Tennessee. It was tough because both of my parents were huge Alabama fans with zero friends who would agree to disagree about their favorite team. My parents had lots of close friends, but when fall rolled around, they became enemies. Everything seemed to give these "so called friends" of my parents the opportunity to perform childish, nasty pranks to our house, cars, faces, etc. even when we weren't playing each other's team. So, instead of having gobs of people gathered together on game day, I have memories of my dad sitting in front of the stereo cabinet blaring Alabama football. Since neither of my brothers ever cared about sports, I saw the perfect opportunity, so I was usually close by during sporting events. I was daddy's little girl, always vying for some attention. I would watch my dad go nuts on every play, while I would try to keep up… trying to imagine in my head what in the world was going on. We attended a few games, but not many due to the long drive from Knoxville to Birmingham. But the games we did go to were very memorable.

I got my first car in 1988 and immediately purchased a University of Alabama sticker and carefully centered and placed it on the back windshield, thinking all along of my college of choice. I moved to Birmingham in 1989 and began my senior year at W.A. Berry High School. I made friends quickly, but I really don't recall having any friends that were Auburn fans except one, Amy Barnette. I'll get back to her. Graduation was approaching, and I knew I had to apply to college quickly. I had procrastinated long enough, thinking all along that it would be no problem to be accepted! I mean, I was a third generation legacy. In addition, upon my grandfather's death, a scholarship was set up in his name, so no problem, right? WRONG! I completed the proper paperwork, mailed it off and was rejected! What, I thought! Who do they think they are? All of my family lives in Tuscaloosa, most of my cousins close to my age had just graduated, the scholarship, my parents... what is the problem here?

Angry and determined, I persisted and made an appointment with the Dean of Admissions to find out what the problem was. I admit my grades weren't great and my ACT score not the top of the ranks, but I had seen many of my friends get accepted with lower ACT scores and grades than me, and I didn't understand. I arrived at Rose Hall several minutes late. I was only familiar with three areas of Tuscaloosa at this point: the bars, the fraternity houses and the residential areas, so the campus was foreign to me. I did call to ask for better directions and made the secretary aware of my tardiness due to my poor directions. But apparently my 15-minute delay cost me a college career at The University of Alabama. Or maybe it was my grades. Either way, I had never been so disappointed in my life. But, it changed my life.

That summer I spent most of my waking moments in Auburn. Remember my friend Amy Barnette? She was accepted conditionally to Auburn and had to attend summer school and prove herself in order to attend Auburn unconditionally. Amy didn't have a roommate and didn't know anyone down in Auburn yet, so being the friend I am, I chose to be her guest at every party Auburn had that summer. I was life guarding probably 30 hours a week, but every time my shift ended, I immediately hopped in my car and headed south down Highway 280. Every paycheck went to gas, drinks and the famous late night food trips.

By the end of the summer, I had met so many nice people.

Everyone seemed to be pretty genuine and kind, not pretentious, or snobby. I began to reflect on the parties that I had been to at Alabama and realized the vast difference! The girls at Alabama were awful. Actually, I never made any female friends there, if that tells you anything.

I had begun the transformation by the end of the summer. That summer will stay in my memory forever. I didn't really accept my conversion yet, but, unbeknownst to me, it was all in "the plan." I began my college career at the University of Montevallo. I joined a sorority and found lots of friends who were Auburn fans. I continued to frequent Auburn with them on the weekends. Montevallo was what we called a suitcase college. Everyone packed up and went home on the weekends, except those of us who chose to experience college to its fullest, but the fullest experience was not going to be in Montevallo. We would pack into a few cars and head for "the full experience" in Auburn.

After the first semester at Montevallo, I met a guy who happened to have been raised in Auburn. His dad was a professor at Auburn University and his mom was a teacher at Auburn High School. He had a wonderful family living right in the heart of "The Loveliest Village on the Plains." We dated for several months and the transformation was almost complete.

Soon after, I met a new boyfriend (now husband). At this point I didn't have a choice. When I met his family, the conversion was complete. When planning our wedding, I mentioned Labor Day weekend as a possible date. They thought I was kidding, "Who would plan a wedding during football season?," they said. So we got married in May. I realized after going through one football season with "The Family" that there was no turning back. Dye-hard is an understatement when you refer to this family. It is similar to the mob... once you are "In"... you are "In"... chances of getting out would probably involve something with the witness protection program.

We have cut a few family ties in 9 years of marriage but there is one tie that is made of steel... the tie to the "The Auburn Family." And you know, all kidding aside... I put away that set of wire cutters years ago.

War Eagle!

Elise Renzetti
Birmingham, Alabama

Jordan-Hare Stadium

"I made it inside the gate and started up the dark tunnel. …I made it through the tunnel into the light and could see the vibrant green field; all of the players, coaches, cheerleaders and the fans fired up and ready to march into victory. At this moment, a feeling of complete exhilaration and emotion took over. A feeling that made the hectic morning journey all worthwhile. A feeling that I can only describe as goosebumps."

– David Kessler

GOOSEBUMPS!

I was running late. I didn't mean to, but I got in late the night before. That is when I got the message that they had an extra ticket. I had to meet them in Auburn before the game to pick up my ticket. But that meant I had to get there first.

If I could have woken up earlier and beat the crowd! But I didn't, and so I was sitting on Highway 280, 10 miles south of Alexander City, in standstill traffic. I prefer evening games to morning or night games. I'm not crazy about getting home so late, but I like to do some tailgating before the game. That wouldn't happen that day; I was watching my tailgating time slip by with the idling of my engine.

Finally, I got to Auburn, but I had to park so far away I couldn't even see Jordan-Hare Stadium. I was even on the other side of the tracks. I had to run. They probably wouldn't wait for me because they liked to go into games really early. I sprinted by all the familiar sights: Daylight Doughnuts, Cheeburger Cheeburger, Mellow Mushroom, Finks, Denarios and Toomers' Drugs. I normally would have loved to take my time, walking through that area and bringing back all the great memories. But I didn't have time or the trip would be in vain. I slipped behind Samford Hall and finally made it to their tailgating spot. They had already left. And so had my ticket. There was nothing left but cars … no food, no drinks, no tents and folding chairs, nothing. I wondered if I could even find a ticket now. There were droves of people walking by me. All happy. All looking forward to kickoff. All With their ticket in hand.

I remembered a game the previous year. There had been a similar situation. A guy was running late to one of the games and was trying to meet us to get a ticket. They left the ticket at the car, behind the tire. He never found it. I remembered thinking that I couldn't be that lucky. I was even amazed that I had remembered it. I looked there just in case, and, lo and behold, there was my ticket. Instant joy!

I ran down the rest of the concourse and across the parking lot to Jordan-Hare. I was in line, waiting to get through the gate. People were all around, just squeezing in trying to get through. I was standing there, covered in shadows. The wind was blowing, and I realized that I was actually cold. I could hear the band playing. I could hear the all too familiar sound of the fans getting louder, and then the thunder as the team ran out on the field. I was so close now. It always seems like forever when you are missing something. I made it inside the gate and started up the dark tunnel… I made it through the tunnel into the light and could see the vibrant green field; all of the players, coaches, cheerleaders and the fans fired up and ready to march into victory. At this moment, a feeling of complete exhilaration and emotion took over. A feeling that made the hectic morning journey all worthwhile. A feeling that I can only describe as goosebumps.

David Kessler
Birmingham, Alabama

Tiger Walk Entrance into Jordan-Hare Stadium

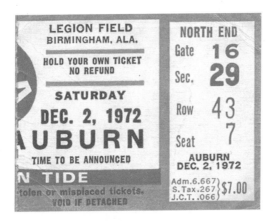

"Ticket Stub from Auburn vs. Alabama — December 2, 1972"

"I'm 50 years old now, and I've seen some exciting things in my day, but nothing will ever top December 2, 1972, Legion Field, Section 29, Row 43, Seat 7."

— Donald Thorton

SECTION 29, ROW 43, SEAT 7.

"Auburn vs. Alabama – December 2, 1972"

I'm 50 years old now, and I've seen some exciting things in my day, but nothing will ever top December 2, 1972, Legion Field, Section 29, Row 43, Seat 7.

It was there that I experienced the greatest thrill of my life. And I'll never forget it, because Auburn did the impossible that day.

My father, a 1949 Auburn graduate, was at my side. For most of the game, Auburn appeared to be unable to generate any offense. To make matters worse, an Alabama fan sitting in front of us was being particularly obnoxious. He was drinking more than just coke, and it was obvious.

With just over five minutes to play Auburn faced fourth down in Alabama territory, and Coach Ralph "Shug" Jordan sent in the field goal unit. I must admit, I was embarrassed, and I didn't want to lose 16 to 3. I wanted a touchdown just to prove to the drunk Bama fan that we could score.

But then things changed. And what transpired in the next five minutes was the greatest, end-of-the-game comeback I have ever witnessed. It's pretty rare to block a punt, recover the ball and score a touchdown. But Auburn did it twice in a matter of minutes.

When David Langner scored that second touchdown to tie the game, and Auburn kicked the extra point to go up 17-16, the Auburn fans erupted like I have never seen nor heard since. Meanwhile, the Alabama fans sat stunned in disbelief. An Auburn fan sitting next to me poured her coke on the head of the intoxicated Bama fan, and he just sat there. He didn't do or say anything. The celebration that followed seem to last forever. We were so excited, I didn't know if we would ever come down.

That moment was unbelievable. Sometimes I even pull out my old ticket stub and get choked up just thinking about it.

Donald Thornton
Lilburn, Georgia

Beard-Eaves Memorial Coliseum

HOME FROM SAUDI

My husband's U.S. Air Force assignment took us to the Kingdom of Saudi Arabia on a joint command assignment, in which the family was allowed to go along. This was in July 1989. Unbeknownst to us, a year and a month would pass before Desert Shield would begin, and we would all be involved.

The Kingdom is a great place for an Auburn Tiger to visit. You can say, "WAR EAGLE" as loud as you want and feel like King of the Desert, because there is no one to answer, "Go Bama Go!" So, of course, I liked it. The Gold Souq shopping was the best, the day trips around the Kingdom with the youth camp were unique, and it was AUsome to bargain for the beautiful items I wanted in my home, until…

Desert Shield became a reality, as did Desert Storm, with us still there in the Kingdom and no way out. On January 18, the first of many sirens would go off on the compound where we lived, 20 minutes outside Riyadh. If incoming scuds had been detected up in the sky, the local military King Khalid Military Community (KKMC) Air Base would answer with two Ba Booms of patriot missiles taking off to intercept. So I prayed while I huddled under a desk or in a closet with the family for cover and thought of the long, hot Auburn days back when life was peaceful and quiet, yet noisy on game day.

We were able to depart the Kingdom on the Saturday before Super Bowl Sunday in 1991. We flew out just as dusk was approaching over the Red Sea and Egypt on our way to the Torrejon Air Base in Spain. There, we boarded with other moms and children yet another C-130 Cargo plane to take us across the ocean. Landing stateside and finally getting to Montgomery, Alabama, was a relief. I promised myself a trip to Auburn to see a women's basketball game as a reward for getting out of there with my family.

But first, I made sure I visited Jimmy Sprayberry, an attorney who I had worked for, and Trey Johnston at the J&M Bookstore. The following week, seven days to the count, it happened. I had to pinch myself while I sat in my seat in the Coliseum with my kids, because I couldn't believe I was here. I saw Ruthie Bolton and the rest of the AU women's basketball team play.

After the game, I introduced my family to Coach Joe Ciampi and told him of our plight and what this game had meant to me. He gave me a hug, welcomed us home and shook my children's hands. He introduced us to the players and gave my kids AU Women Basketball shirts, which still remind me of our journey back to Auburn. I was again reminded… it is great to be an Auburn Tiger!

Cynthia Sebastian
Wichita, Kansas
Auburn University
Class of 1979

Photo taken by Carol Coffey on the way to 1982-83 AU Speech Team Nationals in Normal, IL (Illinois State U.) In the back is our white van, called the "White Avenger", Back - L to R: Susan (Fry) Mitchel (an assistant coach) and Suzie (Crook) Fergus; Middle - L to R: Ricky Heartsill, Katie Ginanni, John Thompson, Cheryl (Crook) Thompson, and Mark Fowler; Front - L to R: Lena Hegi (assistant coach) and Beth (Langford) Beno.

"Most Auburn fans know the phrase 'Bo over the Top,' have heard many tales about that famous game and have seen the artists' renderings of that moment. But I remember so clearly how 40,000 Auburn fans at Legion Field — and many more at home — went over the top for the score with him."

– Carol Coffey

THE GAME
"Auburn vs. Alabama – November 27, 1982"

Most Auburn fans know the phrase "Bo over the Top," and have heard many tales about that famous game and have seen the artists' renderings of that moment. But I remember so clearly how 40,000 Auburn fans at Legion Field... and many more at home... went over the top for the score with him.

It was 1982, and I was a senior at Auburn. The year before, Pat Dye had been hired as head football coach, a move welcomed by most of the Auburn community. Dye only won five games his first year, but in his second year, the team was heading into the Alabama game with seven wins.

You could tell we were gaining momentum, and a couple of players had already become household names. The main one, of course, was Bo Jackson. Banners saying "Go Bo Go" were all over the student section. And every time Bo got the ball, the crowd would yell, "GO BO GO BO GO BO GO, GO, GOOOOOOOOOOOOOO!"

Just before the Alabama game, Coach Paul "Bear" Bryant announced he would be retiring after the season, which seemed to shock Auburn fans more than Alabama fans. It was almost as if we had to get a win over "The Bear" before he retired, so we could say we beat him in his final game.

Back then, the Auburn-Alabama game was played at Legion Field and often on Thanksgiving weekend. A lot of Auburn people complained about the location, saying that it wasn't a neutral site because Alabama used it as a home field for other games. But after I graduated, I didn't mind, because I lived an hour north of Birmingham and more than three hours north of Auburn, so going to the game on the long weekend was easier when it was in Birmingham.

As the game progressed, Bo Jackson and Lionel James were moving the ball and putting up points. The Auburn side of the field (at that time, each school had 50 percent of the tickets) was getting louder and louder as we got more and more confident. But Alabama didn't just roll over; we had to work for every point and every tackle, but we really had the upper hand most of the game. The difference in that year was we knew that we couldn't lose the game in the last couple of minutes. This had to be our year. And it was.

Today it seems like tearing down goal posts is almost commonplace. But back then it didn't happen much. For one thing, state troopers with big batons hit people who tried. Even though they were down on the field at this game as well, I found out later that they let us all go over the fence.

My friends all headed for the chain-link fence as the clock ran out. There just really isn't a more thrilling feeling than being with all those excited people as the clock winds down, as you realize that nine years of losses are wiped out.

In fact, I believe the people who were storming the field never saw the last second tick off the clock. I, of course, had my trusty Auburn sweatshirt on and orange and blue paws painted on my cheeks. As I got to the fence, a very nice man was helping people over. Being a little punch happy and giggling like a fool, along with about 10,000 other students, I thanked him as he boosted me over and then just hung their laughing as my shirt got hooked on one of the links.

My friends helped me rip my way out of that, so as we ran onto the field, I was basically half naked. The crowd was too thick for us to get near the goal post, but I could see it coming down fast. It only took ten minutes at the most. Coach Dye let the players come back on the field after they had gone to the locker room, and everyone was hugging, kissing and telling them we loved them.

Suddenly the players started moving back towards the locker room and one of my friends and I found we were caught in the middle of about 30 football players. We had to go where they went or get trampled. When we realized they were going back to the locker room, we just laughed and wondered how far we were going to get.

Just as we got to the door, a huge arm reached in and pulled us out of the crowd. A state trooper with a stern grin on his face said he didn't think two young ladies should be exposed to that much testosterone at that point in our lives. We just laughed and were thrilled that we made it that far.

That feeling of exhilaration lasted all the way home to Auburn and during the next week for exams. That was an incredible Auburn experience. And just one of many I have had over the years.

Carol Coffey
Huntsville, Alabama
Auburn University
Class of 1983

"Auburn vs. Alabama — November 20, 1999"
L-R: Norma Jean Marsh, Harold Marsh,
Shannon Marsh Wesley and Tamara Marsh Flowers

"I actually received a scholarship to go to Troy State University, but I turned it down to go to Auburn. I did not tell my parents about the Troy State scholarship until I had been at Auburn for three years. I did not want to take the risk of them making me go to Troy State."

— Shannon Marsh Wesley

MY LOVE FOR AUBURN

There was never any doubt that I would go to Auburn. Ever since I was a young child, I knew Auburn was the place for me. Part of the reason was that my sister, who is two years older than me, was already there, and I wanted to go where someone could help pipeline me into the social life.

I actually received a scholarship to go to Troy State University, but I turned it down to go to Auburn. I did not tell my parents about the Troy State scholarship until I had been at Auburn for three years. I did not want to take the risk of them making me go to Troy State.

I have always loved Auburn, but one thing is for sure; you love it even more once you get there. I was in Pi Beta Phi sorority and loved all of my friends. I had a job at Foy Union. Part of the tradition was that you could call Foy anytime and ask them anything. And trust me, people did! In our job description were the words, "Don't ever leave a question unanswered." Of course they never said it had to be a correct answer. (Only kidding!)

I remember the two most asked questions were, "How many bricks are in Foy Union?" and "How many bricks are in the concourse?" I do not remember either answer now, but I bet you can call Foy yourself and find out. We had the reputation of always being there, even on game days. You would be surprised at the number of people who would call and ask us to do their homework for them. They'd say, "I'm stuck on this math question...can you help me?" I did not always know the answer, and it was not always easy to find.

We had a bookcase behind the desk with everything from encyclopedias to Auburn fact books, maps and charts with all kinds of formulas in them. I understand it is easier now because they have computers and you can just access the Internet. Frequently, I would have to call a friend or my sister to find some of the answers. One time someone called with a unique question. The person needed to know the name of the thing you use to shock people back to life. The answer was a defibrillator (I was also working at the hospital). But if you didn't have the answers, you would call someone who would know. It was like using a lifeline.

In addition to my Foy experiences, there were many other things I loved, like Chawaukla Creek and tailgating parties. I loved the parade before the Georgia game and that feeling at the beginning of a game day and after we won. I remember the 1994 Florida game. We watched it at my apartment, and after we won, we took off to roll Toomer's Corner. As we were running by McDonald's, the people working there came out and gave us the toilet tissue out of the bathroom and said, "We can't get off work, but go roll it for us!"

These are the kinds of things that make Auburn great to me, and everyone else feels the same way. Everyone pitches in and is just happy to be there. You can't put into words all the reasons you love Auburn (or at least I can't), but you just know it.

Shannon Marsh Wesley
Birmingham, Alabama
Auburn University
Class of 1996

"Tiger Walk – Sarah, Sloan and Jim"

"Jason and Denise Shaw – 2001"
"Note: 'Kirsten' on the window is the daughter
they were pregnant with in 1989"

*"I finally found one (a ticket to
the 1989 Auburn vs. Alabama game) –
it was $125, which was more than I wanted
to spend. However, $125 is a small sacrifice
for a happy, pregnant wife."*

– Jason W. Shaw

1989 AND PREGNANT

"Auburn vs. Alabama – December 2, 1989"

I t was the Thursday before Alabama's historic first trip to Jordan-Hare Stadium. I had a ticket to the game, but my pregnant wife did not.

I had a ticket, thanks to the seemingly never-ending generosity of Mom and Dad. I was obsessed with the prospect of finally getting to play Alabama in Auburn and had talked of nothing else for weeks. I was thrilled that I would be a part of history, live and in person.

But I was a newlywed, and my beloved wife, Denise, was four and a half months pregnant, and she didn't have a ticket. And that fateful Thursday afternoon, my lovely wife informed me, and I quote, "You better find me a DAMN ticket to the Auburn game."

I heard her words and understood exactly what she meant. So I embarked on a desperate search for a ticket. I started by calling ads in the paper, but was turned down repeatedly. I gave up on local calls and began calling ANY and ALL numbers that had tickets for sale. I finally found one… it was $125, which was more than I wanted to spend. However, $125 is a small sacrifice for a happy, pregnant wife.

The ticket sellers lived in Muscle Shoals, Alabama, and I was in Alabaster, Alabama. They told me that they were headed to Montgomery, and I could meet them there to pick up the ticket. But, after some real brainstorming, I called a dear friend, Tom Cherry, and asked him to hook up with these people and purchase the marriage-saving ticket for me. Cherry agreed, and, after much searching, finally found my southern-bound saviors and purchased the precious ticket, just in the nick of time, on the eve of the big game.

Now let me remind you again that my wife is pregnant. We left Alabaster at 4 a.m. on Saturday and headed to Montgomery to pick up Tom Cherry (TC) and the ticket. We got TC and the ticket and headed to Auburn. Life was good, and I was a hero.

We tailgated and whooped it up until the Tiger Walk. We got in line with thousands of screaming Auburn fans. I was happy as I could be. Right before the teams walked through, my wife informed me that she couldn't see. Being a good husband and not wanting to upset my pregnant wife, I offered to sit her on my shoulders so she could see and take pictures of the players as they strode by. She agreed, and I placed her on my shoulders. She got some great pictures, and all the players were looking right at her. I guess it's not every day you see a pregnant woman towering above a crowd.

Then it was on to the stadium, where we cheered our beloved Tigers to victory. I was a happy man. All my hard work had paid off. My Tigers had won. I was there to see history. And I still had a wife.

Just goes to show you that with GOD, family, friends and Auburn, life is complete.

Jason W. Shaw
Wilsonville, Alabama
Birmingham, AL

Brian and Mark Stanfield

"1983 Auburn vs. Maryland Ticket Stub"

"I think it was the Maryland game, but it could just as well have been the U.T.-Chattanooga game. I think Boomer Essiason was their quarterback, but to a 12-year-old boy, all football players are stars. What was most important to me at that moment was that it was game day, and I was heading down to the Plains."

— Mark Stanfield

TIGER DAY

"Auburn vs. Maryland – November 5, 1983"

I t wasn't the first time I'd been to an Auburn football game, and it certainly would not be the last. But for some reason, November 5, 1983, just seems to stick in my mind as my first game-day memory.

I think it was the Maryland game, but it could just as well have been the U.T.-Chattanooga game. I think Boomer Essiason was their quarterback, but to a 12-year-old boy, all football players are stars. What was most important to me at that moment was that it was game day, and I was heading down to the Plains.

My dad was famous for his game-day preparations, which were typically well underway long before they really needed to be. He would carefully clean out the car and get all the necessities within reach. The radio was locked into the Auburn pre-game show. The night before, my brother, Tim, and I laid out what we would wear. This was during the Pat Dye era, so you can be sure we were decked out in some of our finest "Dye Hard" gear. My dad was a huge Dye supporter and frequently told us times were changing from the losing streak we had to Alabama in the 1970s. It is great to look back and see that he was right. Since the 1970s, Auburn has the longest win streak against Alabama of four wins. And in the last 21 years, Auburn has won 11.

Before bed, we would organize our shakers, seat cushions, old programs, recruiting guides and tons of other Auburn paraphernalia and set our loot by the front door. We wouldn't sleep a wink because all we could think about was the game. If we did finally fall asleep, it wasn't long before we were roused by the smell of mom's homemade fried chicken and chocolate chip cookies. I could already see us sitting on the back of the car before the game, eating Mom's great cookin' and listening to Jim Fyffe piping through car speakers and portable radios everywhere.

We always took the trip down Highway 280 from Birmingham to Auburn. As we drove, my dad would tell us about some new recruit from Columbus, Georgia, we'd landed, despite the valiant efforts of UGA. We would stop by Hardee's and get a biscuit and a cup of coffee. We didn't really like the taste, but we had to drink coffee to be cool like Dad.

As we crossed the tracks into Auburn, my heart would skip a beat. Then we would wind around to the parking spot we'd chosen for that year, unload and stretch our legs.

The combination of the pre-game hype and the caffeine from the coffee and Cokes would get us so excited we could hardly stand it. We would work out some of the energy by running mini "down-out-and-up" patterns while my dad hit us with his amazingly accurate Nerf football passes.

After pre-game warm-ups, we would go shop for more Auburn gear. Along the way, my dad would point out somewhere he had a class or where he first lived when he started school at Auburn. As we walked along College Street, we'd be handed stickers, or sometimes we stopped to get paw prints painted on our cheeks. Once we reached J&M Bookstore, Anders' or Tiger Rags, we would blow large amounts of our hard-earned allowance. We'd buy a game-day shirt or a tag for the car we didn't have yet. But it really didn't matter what it was, and we never had buyer's remorse, because this was authentic Auburn stuff.

We would head back to the car to drop off our purchases, then start working our way toward the stadium. We would head over to Donahue Drive to hear the Auburn Drumline and watch the monstrous players file into the stadium. Along the way to the Tiger Walk, my dad would invariably point out the location of the old Coliseum, where he saw Auburn play LSU in 19-something, and "Pistol" Pete Meravich scored 50 or 60 points. It's ironic that the old Coliseum burned down later during an Auburn-LSU game.

After the Tiger Walk, we'd go by and see the Eagle's Cage, and then we were off to the game. As we waited to get in, my dad would point out the gate where he got into a 19-something Auburn versus Georgia game on a ticket from the week before.

Then we would grab a souvenir "Coke" cup and peanuts. As we got closer to our seats, I could feel the hairs on my arms rise. When we walked through the tunnel and the light hit my eyes, I would gaze with awe upon the well-manicured field with its slight dome and flowerbeds in the corners of the end zones with a football or Auburn logo.

I'm not one who easily remembers the stats and details of particular games, or even exactly what happened on the defining play. I'm pretty sure that in the 1983 Maryland game, Number 54 Gregg Carr, one of my favorite linebackers, made a heroic stop or two. And thanks to modern technology, I can hop on the Internet and see that Auburn won the game against Maryland on November 5, 1983, a little less than a year after "Bo-over-the-Top" broke Auburn's nine-year Iron Bowl losing streak. Auburn ended the season ranked third in the nation in 1983. They capped off the year with a 23-20 win over Bama and a 9-7 Sugar Bowl win over Michigan.

What I do remember, without the help of technology, is the feeling I got... and still get today... just thinking about any game-day trip to the Plains. My son just turned seven, and I look forward to the day when he can reminisce with me about his first memory of a "Tiger Day" on the Plains. Who knows? Maybe this is the year!

War Eagle!

Mark Stanfield
Birmingham, Alabama

Bailey Stanfield and Aubie
"Team Fever Kickoff Party"
August 2, 2003

"Amy Gerhard boarding a Greyhound Bus
bound for the 1999 Auburn vs. Alabama game"

*"For most of the 86,000 Auburn fans that head
down to the plains for an Auburn-Alabama game,
tickets are the biggest concern. The trip usually
isn't a big issue since they typically live only a
few hours away. For us, however, the trip was a
little more involved. Living in Ontario, Canada,
you don't just get a call from a buddy who has
tickets and head off to the game."*

– Amy Gerhard

24 HOURS TO AUBURN

"Auburn vs. Alabama – November 20, 1999"

I first visited Auburn in 1999 while on vacation with my boyfriend, Phil. We had been dating for eight months, and he had told me all about his trips to Auburn. He said it was his favorite place in the world. He told me how nice everyone is, and how he was certain I would fall in love with Auburn, too. I did fall in love with Auburn, despite the 24 hours it took to get there.

For most of the 86,000 Auburn fans that head down to the plains for an Auburn-Alabama game, tickets are the biggest concern. The trip usually isn't a big issue since they typically live only a few hours away. For us, however, the trip was a little more involved. Living in Ontario, Canada, you don't just get a call from a buddy who has tickets and head off to the game. First we must cross the U.S. border, then catch a Greyhound bus in Detroit, Michigan. Twenty-two hours later, we meet up with old friends in Marietta, Georgia and then head off to the game.

When I arrived in Auburn for the first time, the fans were so warm and welcoming. It was like being part of a family. I got a chance to do a little shopping at J & M Bookstore and Tiger Rags and loaded up on enough AU souvenirs and attire to fill my closet.

Then we proceeded to Jordan-Hare Stadium. Wow! That was so cool! Everybody was tailgating and partying before the game. I felt so close to the Auburn family, like I was one of them. We bought tickets, which were not cheap, and went to the game. It was so wonderful seeing the Auburn fans cheering and yelling "Beat Bama." I knew I was in for the best fun of my life.

Unfortunately, we lost to Bama that year, but that didn't matter to me. It was great just to have the opportunity to get to go to Auburn and actually get to see them play live instead of on the video tapes my boyfriend has collected since the first game he attended on December 2, 1989.

Even though it takes us 24 hours on a bus, it is worth it. We are truly Dye-hard Auburn fans and that will never change. I love Auburn and it will always be very special to me. In fact, now there is no other place in the world I'd rather go on my vacation than Auburn, Alabama.

"It's great to be an Auburn Tiger!"

Amy Gerhard
Sarnia, Ontario, Canada

TIGER'S FLIGHT

Having graduated right before Tiger, the Auburn Eagle, began her majestic soar around Jordan-Hare Stadium, I had been longing to see what all the fuss was about. I finally got to see her in 2001, and I'll never forget it.

I wasn't really sure exactly when the show would start, so I waited anxiously through the pre-game talks and cheers. Finally, I heard the familiar sound of thousands of fans beginning their slow methodic chant of "WAAAAAAAAR..."

I joined in, and as I looked above me, I saw her. She was so regal and poised as she flew rhythmically to the sound of our chant. Circling for what seemed like forever, Tiger finally landed perfectly on the 50-yard line as the fans concluded the chant in unison with a resounding, "...EAGLE ... HEY!"

I will never forget how proud I felt at that moment. I felt tears come to my eyes, and I realized just how great it felt to be an Auburn Tiger. There is no other Southeastern school, or any other college, for that matter, with the pride and tradition that we carry as the Tigers.

War "Damn" Eagle

Kelly K. Davis
Birmingham, Alabama
Auburn University
Class of 2000

"Wedding in Jordan-Hare Stadium"
L-R: Huell Dendy, Ethel Dendy, Heather DuBose,
Stephanie DuBose, Kim DuBose, Susan DeLoach,
Bob DeLoach, Patrick Grainger. Back: Rev. Aldridge

*"In June of 2000, Jordan-Hare was decorated
with orange and blue balloons, making an aisle
out to the center of the field on the 50-yard-line.
I wore a wedding gown and carried an
orange and blue bouquet."*

– Susan DeLoach

NEW BEGINNING AT JORDAN-HARE

I n June of 2000, Jordan-Hare was decorated with orange and blue balloons, making an aisle out to the center of the field on the 50-yard-line. I wore a wedding gown and carried an orange and blue bouquet.

My three daughters were attendants, with the two youngest in orange dresses and the oldest in blue. They carried blue flowers with orange and blue ribbons. My husband and his best man wore Auburn ties that played the Auburn fight song.

We also had special wedding favors for the guests: Auburn tiger head key chains that played the Auburn fight song. After the ceremony and we were pronounced husband and wife, everyone pressed their key chain, and the fight song rung out. It was great!

The reception was a tailgate party at the Eagle's Cage, catered by Country's Barbeque, of course, and complete with all the tailgating food our guests could eat. And our three-tiered wedding cake was decorated with orange and blue icing.

Everyone wore casual, comfortable clothes, and the children loved being in Jordan-Hare. Of course, most everyone there was an Auburn fan, so it was truly a memorable experience for all. Unfortunately, several Alabama fans declined our invitation, even after my husband told them there would be a special section just for them.

Now, it's been two years since our new beginning at Jordan-Hare and we are so happy! Everyone still talks about what a great experience it was and how much fun we had.

Today, I am a HUGE Auburn fan and watch all the football games that I can't attend. When we first talked about the wedding, we both agreed that it would be great if we could get married in Jordan-Hare Stadium. So, I contacted the Auburn Athletic Department and they were so helpful and nice. The rest is Auburn history.

Now, every time we watch Auburn play on television or go to the game, we are reminded of how we started our new life together. Thank you Auburn for making our special day so wonderful!

WAR EAGLE!

Susan DeLoach
Macon, Georgia

"Auburn 2003 Spring Practice"
Roy Hendrix, Tommy Tuberville and Anthony Love

AUBURNITIS

"Auburn vs. Florida State – October 20, 1990"

B ack in the days when Auburn used to play Florida State in its regular season, Auburn just seemed to have a way of losing those games in the final quarter. We prayed and prayed that it would turn out good in 1990. And it did! The only problem was it started "Auburnitis."

We really wanted to beat the Florida State Seminoles in 1990, especially after a 14-22 loss at Tallahassee the year before and a heartbreaking 7-13 loss in the Sugar Bowl to end the 1988 season. Our prayers were answered when Jim Von Wyl made a last minute field goal and beat the mighty 'Noles, 20-17. Everyone was going wild, and began enthusiastically returning the hatchet chant back to the stunned FSU fans. Frank and I joined the crowd and had a great time. When we finally left the stadium, we passed many FSU fans who were all out of the "hatchet" chants we had suffered over and over until that field goal.

The next day I woke up without a voice. I went to my ENT, and he declared I had laryngitis. After several close games that season, and examining many patients who experienced the same symptoms after every weekend, Dr. Boyd began diagnosing the throat condition as "Auburnitis." Folks called the Tigers the "Heart Attack Team" that season because of all of the "squeakers" we had that ended with a win. Coach Pat Dye gave a lot of credit to the fans, and we felt like we certainly did our part.

I continued to lose my voice after cheering the Tigers on each weekend. This became really embarrassing at work every Monday, because I make my living by talking to people all day long. I managed to get by at work. My ENT, Dr. Edwin Boyd, warned me that I could do permanent damage to my vocal cords, but I could only think that it was worth it. The doctor finally asked me if I could just go to a game and quietly say "War Eagle". I simply replied, "NO—I am an Auburn fan."

Clare Haynes
Birmingham, Alabama
Auburn University
Class of 1978

John Lavoy and Phil Savage

"I think this makes me the biggest Auburn fan in the country — Canada, that is."

– Phil Savage

CANADIAN TRANSFORMATION

"Auburn vs. Alabama – December 2, 1989"

I am from North Bay, Ontario, Canada, but in 1989, I headed south to play baseball at Enterprise State Junior College in Enterprise, Alabama. 1989 was also the year I became an Auburn fan.

Coming from hockey country, I knew very little about college football and the significance of rivalries. My baseball teammates quickly taught me what it meant to live in Alabama; you either love Auburn or Alabama.

This still meant little to me until my best friend took me to an Auburn football game against Louisiana Tech. Auburn won, of course, and "rolling" Toomer's Corner was great. But what really won me over were the people. Everyone was so friendly, and the passion they had for Auburn football was more intense than anything I had ever seen.

On our way back down to Enterprise, my friend said that if I thought that was fun, we should come back for the Alabama game, since it would be the first time the game would be played in Auburn. A few weeks later I asked my friend if we were going to that Auburn-Alabama game coming up in a couple days. He said that he was joking about going to the game because it would be impossible to get tickets. I told him if he would drive, I would get us tickets.

For the next couple days, I begged and begged until he finally agreed to go. "At least we will be there for the game, but we won't be able to find tickets," he said.

So we went, and, as I promised, somehow we got tickets right in the student section! It was truly indescribable, and rolling Toomer's Corner was like a snowstorm from back home. To this day I have a huge photograph of the scoreboard's "30-20" on the wall in my living room.

Since that incredible day, December 2, 1989, I have not missed an Auburn – Alabama game. I have had to take the bus down a few times, but I have not had to walk to the Plains — yet!

I think this makes me the biggest Auburn fan in the country — Canada, that is.

"It is truly, great to be an Auburn Tiger!"

Phil Savage
Sarnia, Ontario, Canada

"Auburn in Alaska"
Notice the "AU" flag on top of the tent.
Photo submitted by Charles Heaton of Birmingham, Alabama

"Dexter's Karaoke — Stark, Florida — October 14, 1994"
L-R: Tommy Barton, Tim Stanfield, Dan Saks,
Elliot Pike, Mark Vines and Tim Delong

*"We were cruising along and had just
barely crossed the state line when suddenly
Tim saw something! We slowed down to take a
closer look. It was a dead alligator lying on a
patch of grass right off the side of the road just
beside a little swampy area. ...The first thing
I said was, 'That is an omen!' "*

— *Tommy Barton*

THE OMEN

"Auburn vs. Florida – October 15, 1994"

During the fall of 1994, I was attending the University of Alabama. This was partly due to the fact that I had friends in Tuscaloosa, but more notable because my dad was only willing to pay for me to go to Alabama. I also had many friends at Auburn, and because they were quickly winning me over, I knew it would be my first and last quarter in Tuscaloosa.

Alabama was undefeated at this time and I had four season tickets that needed to be used by a fan that would enjoy them … so I sold them. These tickets were actually pretty good and included all of the remaining home games and the upcoming away game in Knoxville, as well as a couple of extra SEC Championship tickets I acquired. As a result, I had a nice sum of money amounting to $1,800!

The money was burning a whole in my pocket, and I pondered where to begin my spending spree. I seriously considered betting on a bunch of games … for once if I lost I would have the money to pay up. Then something strange happened. The phone rang and disrupted the thoughts of winning some grand amount from a betting pool. It was Tim Stanfield, one of my best friends from Auburn.

During our conversation Tim brought up the upcoming Auburn - Florida game, and I asked what he thought about going down to Gainesville to the game. He said that Auburn was a 16-point underdog, so it didn't look too good. Plus, he was broke. I understood his financial position, however, I told him about this funny feeling I had that Auburn was going to win. Not just cover, but WIN! After persistently reassuring Tim about my feeling and getting close to begging, I finally could tell his wheels were turning. I hung up the phone feeling confident Tim would pull through and make the trip happen.

Maybe 15 minutes later, the phone rang again. It was Tim with a plan. He had rounded up some other friends of ours from Auburn. The plans were set. Mark Vines, Tim DeLong, Tim Stanfield and myself would be headed on a road trip to Gainesville. Two other friends, Dan Saks and Elliot Pike, planned to meet us later, in Stark, Florida, since they couldn't leave quite as early.

We decided to leave early Friday morning because it was such a long drive. I was in Tuscaloosa, but I was so excited that I still arrived at Tim's apartment in Auburn just after sunrise. I had a great Jeep Cherokee at the time, and we loaded it down with all our stuff for the weekend. In fact, it was so packed, I could barely see out of the back window. We gathered a wide variety of music for the long road trip. Tunes ranging from Jimmy Buffet to Coolio's, "Ganster's Paradise," as well as AC/DC, Van Halen, the Steve Miller Band …and all kinds of great party songs. The weather was awesome, so with the sunroof open and the stereo loud, we got on the road.

I could tell from the beginning that I was the only one feeling confident about winning the game. We were about to travel 10 hours, and I realized that I had my work cut out for me. I knew I had to convince these guys to believe as I did. I kept telling them that, "Not only is Auburn going to cover the line, but we were going to beat 'em." It wasn't just a call, like, if this happens and that happens, we have a shot to win. "No!" was my emotional response to each negative statement about Auburn's chances. I continued to declare that we were going to win the game. Tim was really coming around and began to believe more and more. Mark, however, didn't understand why we were even bothering to go. As for Tim DeLong, I think he was just happy to be there.

We were cruising along and had just barely crossed the state line when suddenly Tim S. saw something! We slowed down to take a closer look. It was a dead alligator laying on a patch of grass just off the side of the road just beside a little swampy area. It was belly up and appeared almost cartoon-like, all it needed was its tongue hanging out and X's over its eyes. The first thing I said was, "That is an omen!" It's not everyday you see a dead alligator on the side of the road, especially on the way to play the Gators. Then Tim S. turned to Mark and said, "It's on! We are going to win! We have seen... 'The Omen'." We even thought of every way possible to mount this monstrous alligator on the car somehow, but never did. That moment completely turned it around. Everyone was really excited to be going now. In that instant we all believed that the sight of that dead alligator forecasted "The Gators" defeat.

We got back on the road and needless to say; by this time we could hardly contain our excitement. As a result, I thought it was a perfect time to let them know about the money I acquired. I casually said, "Guys, we are going to do it right ... and this trip is on me." With their curiosity soaring and questions firing, I pulled out my G-roll of cash. The bills were all crisp hundreds, as if they had been starched and pressed. The guys were speechless, while I explained to them how I got the money. I could see everyone instantly relax, considering the many conversations of trying to figure out the details of how we would split the cost of gas, and rooms. Several I.O.U.'s from Tim S. were beginning to accumulate and were obviously cleared by the good news. It's not everyday you get a trip bankrolled when you are in college, and I wanted to do it up right.

We finally arrived in Stark, Florida where Mark had reserved a couple of rooms. Stark is a "hole-in-the-wall" little town about 30 minutes outside of Gainesville. As we pulled up at the Best Western, we were hungry and very thirsty. We had no consensus as to where to eat, so as Mark went to check in, we discussed our plans. Tim S. mentioned he wanted seafood, but I was in the mood for a big steak. Mark came out of the office and we headed for the room. As we were unloading the Jeep, there it was ... an illuminated sign that read, "The Steak, Seafood, and Pasta Bar ... Karaoke Tonight." It was no further from the hotel than walking across a Wal-Mart parking lot. Perfect!

We chilled out and continued to talk about how cool the stuffed gator hood ornament would have been as we waited for Dan and Elliot. They obviously found our room and knocked on the door. They had worked up an appetite as well, because the first thing out of their mouth was, "Are you guys in the mood for Italian?" We replied, "No, but we found the perfect place." We all made sure we were decked out in our Auburn clothes and walked to the restaurant.

Expecting a little taunting, Tim S. gave us a talk on the walk over to the restaurant. His big thing is to always kill them with kindness. He reminded us, "They are going to say whatever they can to get under our skin. Let's not let them. Let's be nice and cordial, and out-class them the way only Auburn fans can." He reassured us several times that he knew we could do it, regardless. Believe it or not, that was our attitude that night.

We had barely set foot inside when we heard the entire crowd doing the gator chomp in unison and all eyes were on us. The place held at most 40 people, and that would max the fire code. We were instantly faced with 34 enthusiastic Florida fans who had already taken up residence for the night. The hostess put us in a big booth right next to the door, as if to say, "You are going to need an escape route." It was immediate taunting. Some of the things they were saying were amazing. Things like, "Why did you even drive down here? … You have no chance. … We kill people at home. … Have you ever been to the swamp? … No? … Oh, you're in trouble. You should just turn around and go home. … You kids can't handle it. … We've heard of people committing suicide after leaving the swamp." It was bad, much worse than we expected. However, we stayed strong and maintained our class.

We ordered mountains of food and a choice beverage or two. The food was great! Just as we were finishing up, the sheriff (off-duty) walked over and sat down with us. With a kind voice he said, "I just want to tell you that it could be bad and we don't want any trouble in here. All the fans in here… all of these guys and those girls, are going to try to start trouble with you. Be better than that. Don't do it. We love having you here. I have watched you in here and see that you're taking it from them and not returning it. You guys have a lot of class." He handed us his phone number and said, "If anything happens, call my office and ask for me."

We could have left just then but considering it was karaoke night we decided to stay. Tim, Dan and I used to go to this Chinese restaurant to sing karaoke from time to time and became addicted to it. So as we were sitting back in our chairs patting our bellies, we watched them put the last few pieces of equipment together to get the show going. We all agreed that we wanted to sing, but with a house full of Florida fans we were a little timid at first. We watched them sing a few songs. They weren't great really, but we clapped for them anyway, in attempt to keep the peace.

After a couple of drinks, and confidence setting in, we were about to submit our song request. But before we had a chance, someone called us out. They asked, "Oh what … are ya'll too good to sing?" So we decided to put in "New York, New York" (in appreciation of the crowd's Yankee lineage). That was Dan's song. Tim and I went up there with him. It was as if the instant he opened his mouth, they started booing us until the song was over. You couldn't even hear Dan over the constant booing, and Dan is good. I remember during one of the instrumental parts Dan asked if we should just sit down. We said, "No, we have to keep going." The crowd reacted like a bad act on stage at the Apollo. Trying hard not to feel defeated, we headed back to our booth. They kept taunting us, so we continued to drink.

A little time had passed, and I was feeling real good. I think we all were. The atmosphere had reached the feeling of a cold war. We just refused to give in and let them make us feel bad. I turned to Dan and said, "Let's do, 'You've Lost that Loving Feeling.'" Dan agreed, and we put in our request. While waiting our turn I called out to our waitress and asked her to count up all the people in the bar. She did a quick scan and said about 25 or so. Our turn came up and we made our way to the stage. They immediately started booing again. I told the DJ, "Don't start the music yet, but give me a microphone." I got on the microphone and said; "You know … we made a long trip down here. We obviously came down for the game, and have taken abuse from everyone in here. And, honestly, we really don't like it. So, I tell ya what. If I buy the entire bar a round of drinks … can we all just get along?"

As I finished talking, our waitress and three other people appeared and an enormous roar came from the crowd. Each waitress was awkwardly carrying a huge, tabletop sized tray loaded down with overflowing mugs of beer. I feel certain the trays weighed at least a hundred pounds apiece. The beer was dispersed quickly as our song got underway. From that moment on, we were the hit of the show! We had these Gator fans screaming and clapping for us the rest of the night. We snuck in the Auburn fight song and even had a few of them saying, "War Eagle!" before we left. I must have bought the whole bar a second round of beers in there somewhere, because my tab ended up being around $400. It was so incredible and worth every penny. As I paid up we said goodbye to our newfound friends and stumbled back to our rooms, with the "I love you man!" attitude.

Morning came all too soon as we woke up to the alarm clock that Mark had somehow remembered to set. Since kickoff was at 11 a.m., we made sure we had plenty of time for pre-game preparations. We got ready, loaded the car back up, checked out of the rooms and went for a bite to eat.

We were stopped at a red light just inside Gainesville and witnessed another omen. Tim S. looked up as we waited for the light to change. He saw a familiar car and some familiar faces pass through the intersection just in front of us. It was his uncle Alan, his brother Scott and his dad. What are the chances of that? It was pre-cell phone days, so we honked like crazy to get their attention. As soon as they noticed us they pulled into the gas station just ahead of us. We made arrangement to meet up later at the "Tiger Walk" and gave them a big War Eagle!

After breakfast at Denny's, we walked around campus for a while. As we approached the "Tiger Walk" we could see that

THROUGH THE EYES OF A TIGER

the crowd was huge and roaring with excitement! I think Aubie was excited too. He borrowed (without permission) a cop's bicycle and was getting the crowd fired up with his antics, as the intensely focused players made their way through the walk. It was evident they all knew what had to be done. Once the team was in the stadium, the crowd cleared out.

We left the Tiger Walk and split up since our tickets were not together. Mark, Tim S., Tim D. and I sat together in the upper deck, and Dan and Elliot sat down where "the catch" happened. Our location wasn't that bad. We were in the "sunshine seats" and it seemed like you could touch the sun. It wasn't too hot that day, but the sun was beaming down on us. I think we all got a little sunburned.

The game was everything I had envisioned it to be. Auburn hadn't used a tight end all year, and Andy Fuller was amazing. Every third and seven or third and eight ... there was Andy Fuller. He would catch the ball and be wide open. Sometimes he was good for eight yards, sometimes 20 yards. You would have thought he was invisible. And I don't know how, because he was the biggest man ever. From the upper deck, Fuller looked like a monster compared to the other players. I don't know if he was really that big or if he was just so wide open. Whenever, they threw to him there would be no one within 10 yards of him each time he caught the ball. He must have had 10 catches that game for at least 90 yards each.

Later, when we watched it on television, the announcer said that he believed it was going to come down to whoever had the ball last.

With less than two minutes to go we got possession of the ball on our own 20-yard line. The offense methodically drove the ball down that field. There were several fourth-down plays in that drive. Thomas Bailey dived, full length out, and caught a fourth and 10. Frank Sanders dived and got a fourth and 10. Over and over, they were making huge plays to keep that drive alive. It wasn't easy, mind you. We were using forth downs just to make it. The fans on both sides were clinching their teeth, and biting their fingernails. Everyone in our section was jumping up and down so much I'm surprised the stadium seats didn't collapse beneath us!

It seemed like there was no way we could lose. We had proven all day that we could score on them. Auburn fans were going crazy while Gator fans everywhere were quiet in anticipation. The gator fans silence ceased, when Auburn crossed the 50-yard line. Their side started making noise like I've never heard. It got loud … really loud.

We were down by four points, so obviously a field goal wouldn't help. We had to have a touchdown. It all came down to that last play. Third and goal from the eight-yard line with less than 30 seconds left. Frank Sanders lined up. The ball was hiked. Patrick Nix stepped up in the pocket and slow rolled left. Frank dragged the whole field with him. The ball was thrown, and seemed to be in the air about an hour, maybe an hour and a half. It was like time stood still. I grabbed Tim and Mark in a bear hug death grip while the ball was in the air. It was the highest jump I have ever seen a human make. It looked as though Frankie's shoes were as high as the Florida player's belt line. There was one Florida player who jumped up with him, but it was like a classic basketball move, and Frank had boxed that guy out. The ball was thrown high. It was a designed "go up and get it" ball. They knew they had another chance at the end zone because it was third down. But Frankie came down with it. Touchdown Auburn! I could only imagine the voice of Jim Fyffe at that moment.

We were all crying and jumping and going nuts. It was pandemonium. Seeing thousands of Florida fans get up and know that they had been defeated was the greatest feeling. We didn't even see our final kick off. They could have run it back and scored. I don't think we would have even known. It was over to us. All shakers were destroyed and ripped out. Anything in your hand was ringed out and clenched like the rest of your body. Mark Vines' shaker had about seven little strands left. He had even chewed the handle down to a nub.

I had let the guys know at half time that I had placed three friendly straight-up wagers: $500 on Auburn, $500 on Alabama versus Tennessee and $500 on Colorado. All three covered. After the game, I told everybody, "Really guys, don't worry about it. I just won $1,500." So in other words, our trip was not only covered but I still had quite a bit left over.

After the game was over, we were coming down the ramp, singing, "It's Great to be an Auburn Tiger." The entire sunshine section was yelling so loud that I literally thought my head was about to pop off of my body. Everyone was hugging and congratulating each other as we sang.

Once we got to the bottom, there was a huge T-shirt stand. They had printed up a bunch with the Florida score before our last touchdown, but all of those shirts were piled high on the floor. Beside the huge mound of wasted shirts, were people making the ones with the final score as fast as they could... so fast that the shirts we got weren't even right. They were missing the dash between the score. I made my way to the front, and bought 20 shirts. I gave them out to all of our crew first and saved a few for Tim's brother, dad and uncle. I was just throwing all the extras out one at a time to random Auburn fans as we made our way over to where the players come out. We gave Tim's dad, uncle and brother their shirts.

As the players slowly started to trickle out we congratulated each one. It was amazing!

We started walking back towards the Denny's where we left our car. On the way, we passed a hotel right on the main drag called, "The Sunshine Hotel" or "The Gator Inn," or something like that. We all voted unanimously to stay another night, so we got a couple of rooms. Our room had a balcony that faced the street where all the Florida fans had to walk by. We had a huge Auburn flag draped over the side of the balcony. For hours, we kept reliving the best plays of the game and waved at all of the Florida fans who moped by. On occasion we would step back inside, only to hear coverage of the game on ESPN. As we saw replays of the game, we acted as if it were the first time seeing the win! ESPN also included the fact that Auburn was the first SEC team to beat Spurrier in "The Swamp."

One additional thing that made this win so incredible was that Spurrier had reached an unrivaled stage of cockiness prior to this game. He and his players had been talking a lot of trash. Some of the things said were, "We are going to wipe the floor with them" and, "It's just another game for us, they can't expect to come in here and win," and many others. They were overly confident and overly cocky. These types of comments continued to come in even after several facts were pointed out to them such as; Auburn is undefeated. Auburn had an 11-0 season last year, Auburn is still on their streak, Terry Bowden, Bobby's son, is their coach, and not to mention, Auburn beat Florida last year. Spurrier still maintained his stance that they would win at home no matter what Auburn brought. Needless to say, I am sure he wanted to eat his words as soon as Auburn scored the defining touchdown!

The next morning, we decided to paint the windows of my Jeep. I asked the guys to save the back window, as Tim and I were brainstorming to come up with the perfect thing to paint for the ride home. Everyone else painted the score and "War Eagle," but we had to have something better on the back window, something classic, and something that would get under the skin of every Florida fan that saw it. We came up with something really special (without cursing). We told everyone to come around there to see what we had created. We all laughed and knew that would do it.

Although I would love to tell you the message on my back window, I think it better to refrain due to somewhat "suggestive language." Take a guess. If you ever find me at an Auburn game, I'll be glad to tell you.

We departed with the newly decorated Jeep and may have gotten five miles down the road when I got pulled over by the local police. I didn't think I wasn't speeding, but I do have a heavy foot, so who knew? The officer walked up to the window and asked for my license and registration. I said, "Yes sir. Is there a problem? I didn't think I was speeding." He asked me to step out of the vehicle. He escorted me to the back of the vehicle and said, "You know, you'd better be careful down here with your windows painted like that." I responded, "We'll be fine." He then countered, "All right. And I'm not telling you that you have to take it off. But I strongly recommend that you get out of Florida as fast as possible. You shouldn't speed, but you should go directly out of the state."

So we did. We went directly out of the state … only we stopped at every little Florida town on the way back to Alabama to buy their paper with the score printed on it … small souvenirs of our journey.

When we got back to Auburn, it was still crazy, and there were people everywhere. I had never seen so much toilet paper. Toomer's Corner was completely white. It was like Mardis Gras. I dropped the guys off and they asked me if I wanted to wash the paint off. I said, "Nah, I think I'm going to leave it on there."

I headed back to Tuscaloosa. I drove my decorated Jeep all over the campus for at least a week. People were looking at me like I was nuts, considering "War Eagle" was all over it. However, I always got full props from people when they read the back window. Most people said, "Yup, that's for sure."

I will never forget that game, that journey, and my conversion. When Frank came down with the final catch, it was the first time I cried at a football game. I was crying tears of joy. It only meant more to me that I was surrounded by Tim, who had been my best friend forever, Mark Vines and the rest of my friends. And I knew that I would be an Auburn fan forever.

War Eagle!

Tommy Barton
Birmingham, Alabama

"Auburn vs. LSU – September 16, 2000"
L-R: Carrie Lucas, Stacey Inzina, Leigh Casey and Carrie Brown

"*They had this stuffed elephant on a string and a bat. They asked us if we wanted to take a swing at 'Bama.' Leigh got the bat and just beat the crap out of the stuffed elephant.*"

– *Carrie Brown*

NEW ALUMNI KNOWS NO BOUNDS MY FRIENDS, LS-WHO? AND TIM CARTER

"Auburn vs. LSU – September 16, 2000"

Stacey Inzina, Leigh Casey, Carrie Lucas and I had been living together for about four months. Stacey, Leigh and I went to Auburn together, and Carrie went to LSU. Carrie was a friend that Stacey and Leigh had met in graduate school at the University of Montevallo. We found out what a good sport Carrie was when Auburn played LSU in 2000.

The morning of that Auburn game against LSU, we all rode to the game together. We left Birmingham at about 8 a.m. We were all pumped up about the game and really being obnoxious. We had AU magnets all over the car and shakers inside. We had taped the fight song, and, of course, we kept playing it over and over! I'm sure we were driving Carrie Lucas crazy!

When we first got to Auburn, we managed to get the first parking place by Bodega. It was a good sign. We walked around all day and just tailgated with different people that we know. We went into the game fairly early, and being new alumni, we had to sit in the student section, for old times' sake! At the time, it was set up so that once you had shown your ID, they gave you a stamp on your hand. Well, Leigh was going up to people when they came out and asking them to press their stamp against her hand so she could get into the student section. We had to do that four times for all of us to get in, but we did all get in!

We always sat in the South end zone behind the goal post, on about the 20th row. The game went our way pretty much the whole time, but every once in a while the momentum would shift, and Carrie would taunt us. Other than that, we were really letting her have it. She hated us pretty much the whole time. I'm sure she was a little miserable having to sit in the Auburn section, but she was a trooper!

Then LSU had put together a great drive; it seemed like they just made first down after first down. The crowd was pretty dejected at this point, and then LSU got a touchdown. Carrie was giving it to us then!

It didn't last long, because LSU kicked off, and Tim Carter caught the ball in the end zone at the other end of the stadium. We were just sitting there watching until he got to our 40-yard line. We started getting louder and louder as the excitement was building. All I knew was he was running straight toward us, and no one could stop him. We were all going out of our minds. After several broken tackles, Carter got to the end zone and danced sideways right in front of us. He was pointing straight at us as he went by. We were so out of control, jumping up and down and, of course, knocking Carrie all around. We were just screaming and going crazy. Leigh started giving Carrie such a hard time after that. Leigh was shaking her shaker in Carrie's face and telling her to look at the score. I finally told Leigh that we needed to slack off some because Carrie wasn't going to live with us anymore. It was just too soon to test roommates like that. She might even stop being our friend.

After we beat LSU 34-17, we all stayed in the stadium until it seemed like just about everyone had left. Since we were all recent alumni and the band was playing our Alma Mater, we had to stay to listen and sing along. Then the team came back out on the field in their street clothes. They started giving everyone high fives, and we were still going crazy, just dancing on the bleachers and having a good time.

Some newspaper guys even started to take pictures of us. We didn't really think of it at the time, but a couple of weeks later we noticed a picture of all of us in the window at Alpha Graphics. It was a great picture, too. We were all cheering, and Carrie was kind of in the background with a slightly disgusted look on her face.

But back to the story. After leaving the stadium, we went to Toomer's Corner. Of course, we had to take Carrie up there and sing cheers the whole way. On the way to Toomer's, right outside of Haley Center, there were these guys that were so pumped up about the game. They had this stuffed elephant on a string and a bat. They asked us if we wanted to take a swing at "Bama." Leigh got the bat and just beat the crap out of the stuffed elephant.

Later that night we were all tired and didn't really want to go out, and Carrie Lucas was the one who said, "Come on, I'm the one who lost here. And I'm the one who wants to go out. You guys won, and you want to go home and go to bed?" All in all, she had been a good sport the whole day. It was certainly a great day, and I will never forget Tim Carter running straight at us.

War Eagle!

Carrie Brown
Birmingham, Alabama
Auburn University
Class of 1999

SINCE "THE BEAR"

I was 12 years old when Alabama Coach Paul "Bear" Bryant passed away on January 26, 1983. It was shortly after Auburn Coach Pat Dye led Auburn to a 23-22 win over Alabama on November 27, 1982. Things have changed significantly since the days of "The Bear."

Now, everyone remembers that 1982 game. It featured Randy Campbell at quarterback and Bo Jackson going "over-the-top." And it also broke Auburn's nine-year losing streak to Alabama in what would be "The Bear's" final Iron Bowl.

Things have been significantly different since the days of "The Bear:"

• Since "The Bear," Bo Jackson won the Heisman Trophy in 1984 (In 2000, Alabama's Freddie Milons didn't). = AU +1.

• Since "The Bear," after discussions about moving the Auburn home game to Jordan-Hare Stadium and after the University of Alabama Coach Ray Perkins said, 'It won't happen,' on December 2, 1989 Auburn defeated Alabama 30-20 in the first Auburn – Alabama game ever played at Jordan-Hare. = AU +1 + infinity.

• Since "The Bear," Auburn is 4-2 at home against UAT (Note: this should not be confused with the fact that AU is 1-0 against The University of Alabama at Birmingham [UAB], a completely separate university.) = AU +2.

- Since "The Bear," Jordan-Hare Stadium has been expanded to become the nation's seventh largest stadium with a seating capacity of 86,063, well ahead of cramped Bryant-Denny Stadium's 83,818. = AU +2,245.

- Since "The Bear," Auburn started the "Flight of Tiger" in 2000. And now, at every home game, 86,063 fans are overcome with sheer emotion as Auburn's golden eagle, Tiger, flies from the upper deck, circles the field and lands in the middle of the field as 85,000 hearts stop for a brief moment overcome with sheer emotion. Tiger even made the Opening Ceremony for the 2002 Olympics! = AU +++++.

(I should note that Tiger, War Eagle VI, has since retired and Auburn's bald eagle, Spirit, has taken over stadium duty. Spirit flew for five games in 2002 as well as a September 11th memorial service before an Atlanta Braves game.)

- Since the final sighting of "The Bear" on the gridiron in 1982, Auburn leads the rivalry 11-10. = AU +1.

- Since "The Bear," Auburn is 2-0 in Tuscaloosa. = AU +2.

- Since "The Bear," Auburn is 2-0 on my birthday, including the 31-27 win over Alabama at Jordan-Hare on November 18, 1995, and the 9-0 win in Tuscaloosa on November 18, 2000. = AU +2.

Well, I guess all I can say is "War Eagle!" And long live the Junction-Boy Legend of "The Bear!"

Anonymous

"Auburn vs. Alabama Party at Jason Cerniglia's -
November 23, 2002"
Top Row L-R: Josh Voss, Anna Voss, Greg Milam, David Ferrell,
Jason Cerniglia, Mark Johnson, Shelly Johnson, Kurt Weselius
and Mark Vines. Bottom Row L-R: Jennifer Plowden,
Shay Skiba, Natalie Springfield, Jason Williams, Mark Skiba
and Jeff Mimbs

*"Unless you've spent your entire life in a cave
in Afghanistan, you would know that Auburn
was 10-0 when Alabama came to visit in 1993.
The miracle probation season was one game
away from perfection."*

– Jason Cerniglia

THE LOCK
"Auburn vs. Alabama – November 20, 1993"

Mark Skiba and myself started to school at Auburn University in the fall of 1993. Turns out, we picked a pretty good year to start attending Auburn. We started going to all the home football games with a group of friends.

We would sit in Section 21 of Jordan-Hare Stadium, which is located in the upper corner of the end zone in the student section. You would think that these would be fairly bad seats, but they actually were not so bad. We sat on the very last row at the very top. We had a very good view of the entire field and stadium. There was a great view behind us, as we could see Plainsman Park, Beard-Eaves Memorial Coliseum, and over the entire southern section of the campus. It was beauty in every direction.

The only thing separating us from that view was a fence with a big "Section 21" sign on it. We would usually stand on the back row and lean up against the fence for the entire game. There was even a little lock on the fence where we sat. I guess someone just locked it on there one day to mark their spot. We used it every game to mark our spot. Each week we invited our friends to meet at "The Lock" to enjoy our vantage point of the game.

Unfortunately, not everyone enjoyed these seats as much as Skiba and me, so every game someone from our group would sit somewhere else. As the season progressed, it was back down to Skiba and me. But to Skiba and me "The Lock" had become a sacred location, which brought good fortune to our mighty Tigers. Week after week we claimed our spot, and week after glorious week the Tigers prevailed.

Unless you've spent your entire life in a cave in Afghanistan, you would know that Auburn was 10-0 when Alabama came to visit in 1993. The miracle probation season was one game away from perfection. As usual, Skiba and I assumed our positions obeying the proven ritual of "The Lock." I must admit that we were a bit shaken when Stan White was injured in the second half. Could the majestic luck have left "The Lock?" Our fears subsided when Patrick Nix (notably fresh off the sidelines) threw a strike to Frank Sanders for a touchdown. Jordan-Hare erupted, and Section 21 was insane. In this crazed emotion and excitement, I picked Skiba up (a little fellow at the time) and threw him in the air, nearly over the fence. Luckily for Skiba (and me), he grabbed the fence, preventing his youthful demise under Section 21. "The Lock" had proven itself faithful once again, and Auburn victorious in a perfect season.

Many times Skiba and I considered going back for "The Lock." It wouldn't be that difficult, smuggle in a pair of bolt cutters, and this lucky charm could have been ours forever. But as I look back now, I feel as if that sacred emblem was left there for Skiba and me. Down the road, I hope that two great friends may find that spot, honor "The Lock," and witness a season as magical as 1993.

Jason Cerniglia
Birmingham, Alabama
Auburn University
Class of 1997

"Auburn vs. Arkansas – October 12, 2002"
Back: Scott Stanfield and Earnest Stewart.
Front: Rebecca Coan, Daphne Cook and Regina Hendrix.

"Auburn 31 - LSU 28 – Baton Rouge, Louisiana –
September 20, 1997"

*"It promised to be everything that it was.
The Run versus The Pass. Collins versus Craig.
LSU versus Auburn… It is truly amazing how
quickly people get out of Baton Rouge
when the home team loses "*

– Tim Stanfield

THE SWEAT PIT

"Auburn vs. LSU – September 20, 1997"

You can always tell when you walk onto their campus. Some belligerent drunk will yell at you as soon as you step out of your car. The smell of beer, crawfish and throw-up overwhelm your senses, filling the muggy hot air.

The year was 1997, and the Auburn Tigers were set to play the LSU Bengal Tigers on the third Saturday of the fall. It must have been 105 degrees that day. The humidity was so high that your clothes just vacuum sealed to your body after about 20 seconds.

If you have never been to Tiger Stadium in Baton Rouge, you may have a tough time relating to the LSU fan base. Their shouts and taunts on opposing teams fans are relentless, and quite honestly, plain tacky. The part that makes the experience so surreal is that it doesn't matter how good or bad their team is, they talk trash like they were Nebraska. The feeling I got was that their fans are like a trash-talking engine that is powered by alcohol and crawfish. These fans are on the same level to me as Alabama, Florida and Georgia fans.

But, back to the game. LSU was supposed to have the best team in the West, and they were already talking about a S.E.C. crown. "The Magic Was Back." Their team was powered by running back Cecil "The Diesel" Collins. Make no mistake; he was the real deal. Auburn had a pass-oriented offense powered by the most versatile quarterback ever to grace the plains of Auburn in Dameyune Craig. This game could have been promoted like a Heavyweight Title Match.

| | Auburn's | | LSU's |
| | Dameyune Craig | vs. | Cecil Collins |

It promised to be everything that it was. The Run versus The Pass. Collins versus Craig. LSU versus Auburn.

It was a back and forth slugfest. The lead changed on numerous occasions. I am convinced that whoever had the ball last that day would have won the game. Lucky for me and the other 15,000 steamed Auburn fans, we came away with a huge victory, 31-28. I remember the players running over to the fans and celebrating with them. I actually helped pull Takeo Spikes into the stands. We were a frenzied group of Auburn fans leaving the stadium. It is truly amazing how quickly people get out of Baton Rouge when the home team loses.

I remember walking out to the car with three friends. This truck full of LSU fans pulled up and started talking trash to one of my friends. I will never forget what I said next. "Don't let him get to you; he's just mad because his dreams of winning a championship are now ruined."

I could see that I had gotten to him (like salt on a snail). He lowered his head and sped off into the night in disgust. What a great moment for me and for the thousands of Auburn faithful that made the trip.

Tim Stanfield
Birmingham, Alabama
Auburn University
Class of 1999

Heath Cobb and Family

Samford Hall – Auburn University
Photo submitted by Cathy Henry

"We finally made it to the stairs of Samford Hall when she said, 'I need to sit down,' and as she fell to the stairs, I grabbed her hand and went to my knee and said, 'I have loved you for quite some time. I would love to spend the rest of my life with you. Will you marry me?' On the second step at Samford Hall she said, 'YES!'"

– Greg Peoples

AN AUBURN
LOVE STORY

Auburn blessed me with the love of my life on a warm May Day in 1995. Soon after we met, she realized that I was "after" her, but she just wouldn't cooperate with my mission.

But I persisted. I would stop by my buddy's house that was conveniently located across the street from where she lived to see if I could catch a glimpse of her. I would see her outside, she would smile and wave, oblivious to how smitten I really was. I would make up things so that I could talk to her, but she always seemed too busy. I would leave flowers, but received no comments. I seemed thwarted at every turn.

Then cupid threw me another roadblock… her growing interest in my roommate. To my utter devastation, they started dating. But, my lucky break came when my roommate went out of town for the weekend. Now this might not sound like the best thing to do, but I had to give it a try. I wanted her to see that I was the guy for her. So, while my roommate was gone, a group of us went out to a local honky tonk, the now-defunct Silver Spur.

Then the moment of truth came. We were on the dance floor two-stepping to a George Strait (her favorite singer) song. I knew that I had nothing to lose, so I leaned down, looked her in the eyes and gave her a kiss. We kissed for what seemed like days, but it was actually only a few seconds. From then on, we were inseparable.

Spring quarter was nearing an end, and we were only days away from finals and the summer break. We would soon go our separate ways for more than three months. She would head for Missouri, and I would go to Atlanta. Our young relationship would be put to an immediate test. But we survived, running up phone bills well over $200 a month, and talking endlessly about our future and our life together.

More than a year later, I had already graduated from Auburn and was working in Atlanta. I came down every weekend to see her in Auburn. But the weekend of October 3, 1997, was going to be a very special visit. I had purchased a beautiful diamond ring for my future wife. I made the last payment on the ring, picked it up and it was wrapped in a little gold box. I was going to try to wait and give it to her later, maybe for Christmas, but I couldn't resist. I got in my pickup and headed down to "The Loveliest Village on the Plains" and home to my heart.

I was really nervous. I pulled up to her duplex on Maple Street, shaking like a dog. I went in and greeted her as usual. We chatted briefly and then I said, "Let's take a walk." This was very uncommon because I didn't like walking, and I had never done that before. She had not been feeling well and really didn't like the suggestion. I begged her, and finally she gave in. We drove down Magnolia Street and parked. We got out and crossed the street, walked by the tree at Toomer's Corner, walked down the sidewalk near the "AUBURN UNIVERSITY" sign and headed for Samford Hall.

I was really nervous at this point. We finally made it to the stairs of Samford Hall when she said, "I need to sit down," and as she fell to the stairs, I grabbed her hand and went to my knee and said, "I have loved you for quite some time. I would love to spend the rest of my life with you. Will you marry me?" On the second step at Samford Hall she said, "YES!"

We were married on June 20, 1998, in Enterprise, Alabama, and on September 9, 2002, my wife gave birth to a bouncing baby boy named Hunter.

I love Auburn, and am I thankful for my wonderful wife and all the great days on the Plains. Auburn holds a very special place in my heart and will always be extremely important to our family. We get back "home" as often as we can to just visit. Auburn gave me the education that I needed for a good career and the opportunity to meet the love of my life. And for that, I am so thankful.

Greg Peoples
Loganville, Georgia
Auburn University
Class of 1996

Wes May and Hobart May

*"If you have never been to Auburn, then
you are missing out on something special.
And for all those that have, 'War Eagle!'
and 'It's Great To Be An Auburn Tiger!'*

— Weston May

GRANDDAD'S FIRST GAME

My granddad has been an Auburn fan his whole life, but he had never seen a live game before 2002. But it was that year when he finally got to see the Auburn Tigers play in person for the very first time. He got to experience what it was like to be an Auburn Tiger, live and in person.

Granddad drove down for the weekend with my parents. We got to the game in plenty of time to see Tiger VI fly and for the grand entrance of the team. I get to see these two events happen every game, and it still brings chill bumps to my arms. He had the same reaction. He was in awe of the 86,063 people that stood up to see these 45 kids run into the stadium.

After winning the game, we proceeded to Toomer's Corner to see a tradition like no other. After Toomer's, we returned to my trailer (O.K. … Who doesn't live in a trailer at least once while at Auburn?). I had gotten him a football autographed by Coach Tommy Tuberville. His eyes lit up like a little boy's on Christmas Day. It gave him so much joy. Just seeing the love that he had for Auburn on that day made me feel so proud to have given him the opportunity to experience that day.

If you have never been to Auburn, then you are missing out on something special. And for all those that have, "War Eagle!" and "It's Great To Be An Auburn Tiger!"

Weston May
Florence, Alabama
Auburn University
Class of 2004

THE TIGERS, THE GATORS AND THE CAT

"Auburn vs. Florida – October 31, 1970"

On a crisp October morning, my soon-to-be wife, her girlfriend, the other boyfriend, and I left the Plains and journeyed to Gainesville, Florida to watch a Halloween homecoming tussle between the Auburn Tigers and the Florida Gators. The girls, being ex-Ft. Lauderdale beach bunnies, had lined us up a place to stay at a friend's apartment, and upon our arrival we found that about eighteen people were to be crammed into a two-room apartment. But that's what college life was really all about anyway.

The thing I remember most about our arrival was that every few minutes someone would knock on the door selling the drugs of choice of the day. This situation would be unheard of on the Plains, but we were broke and had no alternate accommodations. Being the fine, upstanding Auburn citizens that we were, we would never have partaken in such corruptive vices. Unfortunately, the apartment's resident cat wandered into the drug enhanced brownies that some random Gator vagrant had prepared. When we all returned from our night on the town, the poor cat was jumping up into the air and running around in circles. This beast had a crazed look in its eyes, like a blood-thirsty lion ready to pounce on a baby antelope. As I look back, it reminded me of the Killer Rabbit in Monty Python's "The Holy Grail." Needless to say, nobody slept a wink that night worrying about this bizarre doped up cat jumping on us and clawing our eyes out in our sleep.

The following morning, I was happy to see that this misguided kitten was alive and well eating an extra large bowl of cat chow. Comforted by this and anxious to leave our heathen host, we departed for the game.

We arrived at "The Swamp" and proceeded to listen to all the haughty Gator fans tell us how they were going to kick AU's butt. Little did they know that John Reaves and Carlos Alvarez would prove no match for Pat Sullivan and Terry Beasley that day. In the first half alone, the mighty Tigers put 35 points on the board. Beasley scored on an end-around and a twelve-yard pass from Sully, and Sully scored on a one-yard sneak and passed to Mickey Zofko for another score. The Tigers kept the heat on in the second half scoring four more times with two of those coming on 17 and 80 yard passes from Sully to Beasley. When the dust settled, the Tigers had mauled the Gators 63-14 and Beasley had scored four touchdowns. Sully scored one touchdown and passed for 422 yards in the game I rank as the dynamic duo's greatest cumulative effort in an AU uniform.

This great weekend taught me three very important lessons in life. First… Say No to Drugs. Second… Say No to Cats on Drugs. And Finally… It was then, and is now always great to be an Auburn Tiger.

John F. Pack
Irvine, California
Auburn University
Class of 1970

Doug Burk and daughter, Mandy

"I guess I knew as a child what I still know now as a man, Bama fans will always think they are great, but Auburn fans will always KNOW: IT'S GREAT TO BE AN AUBURN TIGER."

– Doug Burk

GROWING UP IN A BAMA FAMILY

I am 49 years old and still don't get it. My older brother went to Auburn and still cheers for Bama. My dad owned a glass company in Auburn, but was the biggest Alabama fan you could ever know. He took me to Bama games while I was growing up, but never Auburn games.

After a while, I grew to really dislike the whole Bama thing. I just didn't like the fans' attitudes at the games and around town. I was always thinking, "You know Auburn people just don't act like this."

I finally got to go to my first Auburn game when I was about 12. My brother and his wife took me to a homecoming game against TCU on October 22, 1966. We sat in the student section, and my brother cheered for TCU! Auburn won 7-6 and… well, I finally came out of the closet and declared myself an AUBURN FAN!

Well, needless to say, I have been the stepchild of the family ever since. When I was around 30, my mom was sitting on the porch on my birthday and said, "I was going to give you money for your birthday, but all you would do is buy Auburn stuff with it, so I am not giving you anything."

My parents have both passed away now, but my sister and brother are still both big Bama fans. I have put a daughter through Auburn who played in the marching band for four years. I still have season tickets and go to all the games. Yep, my sister still goes to the Bama games and still thinks I am the stepchild of the family. I guess I knew as a child what I still know now as a man, "Bama fans will always think they are great, but Auburn fans will always KNOW: IT'S GREAT TO BE AN AUBURN TIGER."

Doug Burk
McDonough, Georgia

"Auburn vs. Georgia – November 16, 2002"
Scott and Lori Parker

"Al and Albert Henry"

"I have to admit that the rest of the family and I thought them a little foolish and crazy, to go so late at night without a place to stay. The fearless and bold duo arrived at The Heart of Auburn Hotel hoping and praying for a room."

– Cathy Henry

A TRIP TO THE PLAINS
"Auburn vs. Alabama – November 18, 1995"

I watched, as my men got ready for an exciting weekend of football. The weekend started with the state playoff game... Guntersville High School playing Cleburne County High in Heflin on a Friday night. The next day, was the game of the year, "The Iron Bowl," in Auburn, on Saturday.

After the Guntersville game on Friday night, Al, my husband, and Albert Henry, my son, decided to travel to the Plains, without tickets for the game. I have to admit that the rest of the family and I thought them a little foolish and crazy, to go so late at night without a place to stay. The fearless and bold duo arrived at The Heart of Auburn Hotel hoping and praying for a room. When they entered the office, the attendant joyfully said, "You are in luck, someone just canceled five minutes ago." They felt very lucky!

After waking from a good night's sleep, the two headed for the Auburn Grille for a delicious breakfast, Auburn fellowship and hopefully two tickets. While waiting for a table, they met a man from Boston at The Grille. They all shared a common interest, not only in Auburn, but also Boston. They had an interesting conversation with the man until their table was ready. When Al and Albert finished their breakfast and proceeded to the cash register, the lady behind the register said, "Your breakfast has been paid for." Al asked her, "By whom?" She pointed to the man in the back booth. It was the man from Boston. This fine Boston gentleman stood and said, "Good luck and War Eagle!" Al and Albert felt their luck grow. All they needed now were two tickets.

They circled the stadium looking for tickets, but the situation looked very grim. Tickets were tight and too expensive for these guys. Feeling doubtless and hopeless, the two headed back downtown. There they happened across a friend from Guntersville, David Reed. He said, "Jim (Whitaker) heard that ya'll need tickets. I'm going to make your day." David presented them with two tickets that Jim had so graciously given them. With great appreciation they took the tickets and headed for the stadium. There they sat in Jim Whitaker's suite with cushioned seats, eating lots of great food and watching the Auburn Tigers defeat Alabama in an exciting game, ending 31-27.

All of this added up to be a great Auburn experience that will always be remembered by three devoted Auburn fans – a son, a father and the mother who enjoyed seeing her men get to go to the game. I have heard this story so many times that I felt compelled to put it into words. I guess that they'll have to read this book to know that I tipped off the entire town to find them tickets.

Cathy Henry
Guntersville, Alabama

"Auburn vs. LSU – October 16, 2002"
Ginger and Steve Porter

Carol (Childs) Collier and Leland Childs – 1986

"When your dad is the voice of the Auburn Tigers, you have a chance to enjoy some unique experiences. My dad, Leland Childs, was the voice of the Auburn Tigers radio in the late 1940s through the early 1950s. I like to say, 'I cut my teeth on the benches at Auburn.' "

– Carol (Childs) Collier

REMEMBERING DAD: THE VOICE OF THE AUBURN TIGERS

"Auburn vs. Mississippi State – October 10, 1953"

When your dad is the voice of the Auburn Tigers, you have a chance to enjoy some unique experiences. My dad, Leland Childs, was the voice of the Auburn Tigers radio in the late 1940s through the early 1950s. I like to say, "I cut my teeth on the benches at Auburn."

I remember we went on a Friday to Starkville, Mississippi, for the Auburn versus Mississippi State game when I was in eighth grade. When we left Montgomery, Alabama, it was a beautiful day ... maybe 70 degrees. After arriving in Starkville, we checked into the terrible hotel where we were staying with the team. I remember there was only one bathroom per floor, so we had to stand in line with our towel and clothes to take turns using the showers with the rest of the guys.

The next morning we had a chance to pile into some coffee shop for breakfast with the team. One of my fondest memories was getting a chance to sit by Auburn's heralded quarterback, Vince Dooley. As you can imagine, to an eighth grade girl I was on cloud nine. I often wondered if I had a chance to see him again, would he remember that day? But I have a feeling that the moment was a little more special to me.

After breakfast we headed off to the game and it was now a chilly 40 degrees. At this particular game, I had the opportunity to sit in the press box with dad. The downside was the temperature had now dropped to a downright bitter 33 degrees by kickoff. And in those days, the wood press box had no heat or air, plus it was open toward the field without any glass covering on the front. So, I'm sure you can imagine how the wind was whipping in and was utterly painful. I remember I was so thankful that my dad's friends, Bill Beckwith and Buddy Vaden, the "spotters" at the time, made me a small pallet under the desk. I don't remember any of the action on the field that day. I was more concerned with survival at the time. My dad later said that was the hardest game he ever called. Looking back at the results, I'm sure it was even harder, considering the fact that this frosty game didn't really seem to decide anything since the final score was a 21-21 tie.

This game was just one of many that I had the opportunity to enjoy with dad. My dad meant a lot to me as well as to numerous others. He was instrumental in creating the first profitable Auburn radio network in 1944. My dad was also the first public address announcer to start the National Anthem at the beginning of a southeastern football game. The next week, Tennessee followed suit with the National Anthem at their game.

For some of you older Auburn fans, you may remember a couple phrases my dad started at Auburn. As the players entered the field he would say, "Heeerrrre Come The Tigers!" At the beginning of the game he would say, "Get'em up for a Big War Eagle! Are you ready? …. I can't hear you?"

So my question to you; "*Heeerrrre* Come The Tigers! ... Are you ready?"

A Big War Eagle to Ya!

Carol (Childs) Collier
Birmingham, Alabama

Justin Wesley, Joseph Couch, Terry Bowden and Jeff Henderson

*"I remember asking him for the picture
and telling him about my new lucky hat…
He jokingly said, 'You look like some idiot
from Disney World.' …And I replied,
'Ah, but I'm winning you games coach.'"*

– Justin Wesley

192

THE HAT

A trip to Ole Miss started a tradition with some tickets and a hat. And though I've retired the hat now, it is still a prized possession because of all the games it and I saw together.

It all started with the very first game in the 1994 season, and we were playing Ole Miss in Oxford, Mississippi. I remember thinking there was as many Auburn fans there as there were Ole Miss fans, in their high school stadium. I remember looking up and seeing this old guy with one of those straw golf hats. He had a couple of tickets sort of attached to the hat by the cloth band that wrapped around it. I thought that was a great idea. I needed to get a hat and attach all the tickets of games I saw to it.

I decided to start it right then and there. I chose a simple Auburn baseball cap. I had just bought it, on sale. So I did it. One ticket. Now you look stupid with just one ticket, but you got to start it somewhere. So…

I actually got to meet Coach Terry Bowden four games into that season. It was a Sunday afternoon, and we were by his office kind of snooping around, and he just happened to be in there. So we got our pictures taken with him. He was undefeated, and we were just as happy as we could be to get a picture with him. I remember asking him for the picture and telling him about my new lucky hat.

He jokingly said, "You look like some idiot from Disney World."

And I replied, "Ah, but I'm winning you games coach."

He actually signed the hat that day, so I couldn't get rid of that hat. We kept winning every game, and every week I had a new ticket to put on the hat. Then we went to Gainesville, Florida to play the number one team in the nation... the Florida Gators. I was staying at the Theta Chi Fraternity House down there, and I didn't want my hat there. It was a prized possession. A friend of mine who was also going down was staying at a friend's house. So I told him to hold the hat, and I would meet up with him.

The hat was there, but I didn't find him before the game. I found him after the game. And we all know how that game goes, but the best thing was the last play of the game. I was on the fifth row up from the bottom, surrounded by Gator fans. Nix threw to Frank Sanders. It was so far into the end zone and was so far forward that it was almost perpendicular to us. The ball was in the air, and our whole section fell down because we were leaning so far forward to try to see it. We all stood up, completely confused. We saw one official with his hands up, and all the Auburn fans were going nuts. The Florida fans are all just sitting down. So I had to buy the tape so I could see the catch. That's my favorite play, because that was the play that I was there for, but didn't get to see.

I just want you to know that hat made it through four years of me going to games. It didn't make it to every game, but it certainly looks like it did. It may have missed three games in my whole career at Auburn.

People kept making fun of me, so I finally retired the hat. And some people aren't too proud of the Terry Bowden signature. It was also signed by Marcellus Mostella and DeMarcus Curry. Now it is my prized possession, displayed proudly in my office.

War Eagle!

Justin Daryl Wesley
Birmingham, Alabama
Auburn University
Class of 1996

"The Ball"

"Meanwhile, a crowd of incoming fans had taken interest in our crusade. I distinctly remember the laughter as I leaned over the rail and dived head first into the thorns of death, while Illia held onto my legs."

– Elliott Pike

THE THORNY ABYSS

A visit to the Plains in 1987 accounts for one of my many great Auburn memories. My parents, my best friend Illia and I loaded up and headed for Auburn. Aside from Illia's incessant rambling of his love for the piggies-in-a-blanket my mother had prepared, the trip down Hwy 280 was fairly uneventful. By the time we arrived at the choice tailgating location, Illia and I realized that we made one critical flaw in our game day preparation. We had forgotten the football.

With little else to do, Illia and I entered the stadium early to watch the pre-game practice. We were most interested in the kickers. We waited for the chance to catch a kick in the stands. That never happened, but another unique opportunity presented itself. We watched one of the kicks sail high into the air and slightly wide-left of its intended target. With a crackling thud, we heard the ball crash into the hedges. We raced to the spot to help retrieve the ball. The trainer on hand, delicately felt around the hedge but could not recover this precious treasure. He looked skeptically at Illia and me stating, "If you guys can get it, you can have it." We naively appreciated his generosity and leaned over the rail racing our hands and arms into the thorny abyss. We soon discovered that it hurt just as much to get out of the hedge as it did going in. With frequent shrieks of pain, we hung in there and kept searching. Illia had the keen eye spotting the ball at the base of the hedge. However, neither of us could reach the football. We needed a plan.

Meanwhile, a crowd of incoming fans had taken interest in our crusade. I distinctly remember the laughter as I leaned over the rail and dived head first into the thorns of death, while Illia held onto my legs. The laughter quickly turned to cheers of admiration as I pulled my blood soaked torso from the hedge. As we took our bows I most remember looking back to the field as a massive Auburn warrior nodded his helmet as if to say "Job well done." Like a scene from "Lethal Weapon," we briefly compared the wounds of our thorn scarred flesh. I'm sure that we both could have used a few pints of blood, but at that moment we could feel no pain. Teamwork had prevailed and we had the official Auburn University practice football to prove it.

Illia and I shared custody of this ball for many years, until tragically the ball developed a serious stress tumor (most guys will know what I'm talking about). The ball now rest peacefully in my utility room. At the time we claimed this prize, we were 12-years-old. We are now 29, but you better believe we'd go back into the thorny hedges for another chance like that.

Elliott Pike
Birmingham, Alabama

"Auburn vs. Ole Miss - Oxford, Mississippi – Novenber 2, 2002"
Back: David Koski, Sr. Front: Patricia Koski, Melissa Koski
and David Koski, Jr.

Melissa Koski's pot belly pig, "Ribs"

"Eli then proceeded to tell me there was some hay out back if I was hungry and wanted it. I quietly took my seat knowing that all of those people who were laughing at that time would soon be shut up by the outcome of that game. Sure enough, we held true to tradition at Bryant-Denny Stadium and won the game 9-0."

– Melissa Koski

A TIGER IN THE RED SEA

"Auburn vs. Alabama – November 18, 2000"

I was at the 2000 Auburn versus Alabama game, and during this time, I was dating an Alabama fan (Please forgive me). At that school up the road, all of the fans like to gather before the game and listen to "The Eli Gold Show." This gathering takes place out in a big open area close to Denny Chimes.

Considering my current dating situation, I ended up there sitting among hundreds of 'Bama fans. Eli started to ramble on and on about the "glory days" of the football program and the soon-to-be-victory for that day. There I was, on that cold rainy day, wrapped up in my tiger print blanket, trying to block out the awful sounds around me.

I tuned in just as Eli began to talk about "the Tigers and their team," when I heard, "Do we have any Tigers with us today?" I was the only one there, but I proudly stood up and yelled "WAR EAGLE!" Eli then proceeded to tell me there was some hay out back if I was hungry and wanted it. I quietly took my seat knowing that all of those people who were laughing at that time would soon be shut up by the outcome of that game. Sure enough, we held true to tradition at Bryant-Denny Stadium and won the game 9-0.

Melissa Koski
Auburn, Alabama
Auburn University
Class of 2004

Lonnie and June Pardue
51st Anniversary - 2003

*Not a day goes by that I don't think
of Auburn… the school, the town,
the students and the tradition.*

— Lonnie Pardue

THE TIES THAT BIND

I enrolled at Auburn in 1949 and graduated in 1953, so Auburn has been a part of my life for 53 years. I will always be tied to this school and its people.

I still go to Auburn regularly and can stand and look at Samford Hall, Langdon Hall and know that they are all a part of me. Not a day goes by that I don't think of Auburn ... the school, the town, the students and the tradition.

There is a country song, sung by Don Williams, "These are the Ties that Bind." Well, Auburn is truly the tie that binds me to all of the Auburn grads and the fans that were not able to go to college.

I am saddened by the names of friends that appear in the "In Memoriam" section of the Auburn magazine. At age 70, I see more and more names of friends and classmates, and I am ever closer to having my name printed there. That will complete the tie that binds for me, but Auburn will live long past my final entry, and I am glad and proud to have had a lifetime of loving Auburn.

Lonnie Pardue
Fairhope, Alabama
Auburn University
Class of 1953

CALLING OUT
THE GREATS

Front yard football is one of my most memorable times as a youth. We had to just step it up a notch and play this game in the street. Yeah, I know, what the heck were we thinking to play football in the streets in this small town? But, hey, it was a Nerf football.

I was about seven or eight years old, and I lived in a small town just outside of Anniston. Being raised an Alabamian, I was forced to pull for the University of Alabama. All of the boys that I played with were mostly older, and if I remember correctly, they all were Alabama fans, even though they mostly liked professional ball. I got a mind of my own at the very adult age of eight. We started to call out who we were… our favorite players. As the others were calling out greats such as Joe Montana, I called out that I was Bo Jackson! Everyone said, "WHAT?!"

From that point on, I have been a Dye-hard, Auburn Tiger 'til the end. No matter where I have lived from Florida, the heart of Gatorland, to West Virginia, home of the Mountaineers, I have remained a 100 percent Auburn fan. I can remember when I lived in Florida, and everyone in Florida was either a Gator or Seminole. I may have been an outcast in my adolescent years, but still, to this day, I see through my Tiger Eyes.

From that point on, I was always "Bo," and wouldn't have ever had it any other way. I was a proud boy pretending to be Bo, running down the side lines (in the street), giving the 'ole stiff arm to anyone that neared, and sporting the cotton, Number 34, Bo jersey with 3/4 sleeves. I had that shirt for years, and I believe my mother ended up sneaking it away from me and throwing it in the trash before I knew it! You know how moms are… they really don't know what a "true" treasure is!

I really wasn't a huge NFL fan at that time, but, due to Bo, I started following the best damn pro player in history. I started watching baseball games, too. I remember watching Bo play for the Royals and treasuring his baseball card. I started collecting baseball cards because of him. I just wish that we all had more memories of him and his greatness. Come to find out, I have an older sister that ended up marrying a wonderful gentleman that played baseball with Bo. I have always thought that was really cool.

It is funny how just one player from such a wonderful school could have such a huge impact on a young man. I have only had one opportunity to be blessed with a trip to Jordan-Hare Stadium. I was about 12 years old in 1989, and it was just against "Pacific," but one of my friends had an extra ticket. Soon after, we moved away, but that memory will always remain in my mind.

David J. Randolph, Jr.
Charleston, West Virginia

"Auburn vs. Florida – October 13, 2001"

"I convinced myself to go by saying to myself,
'You owe it to Auburn after the great win they
had the week before against State.' ...
'Never count the Tigers out' is the lesson
I learned that day. The Tigers believed in
themselves, and so did 86,000 loyal fans.
We had toppled number one.
Who could imagine?"

– Tim Stanfield

WHO COULD IMAGINE?

"Auburn vs. Florida — October 13, 2001"

W hat is it about college football that is so special? For starters, the game is not played for money … at most schools, anyways … which makes it a game played from the heart. These kids are either busting it on the field to try to get to the next level or simply love the game or their university that much.

College football itself is special, but in my book, Auburn football is even more amazing. Sure, I am married, have a job, have built a house and am looking forward to having children one day. All those things are very important to me. But Auburn football matters, too. A lot. Which is why I'd like to spend a few moments reveling in some of the more glorious moments of the 2001 Auburn football season.

The 2001 season did not hold a lot of promise for the Tigers. "Auburn is losing 90 percent of their offense," I heard over and over again. Did people forget that we won the S.E.C. West last year? Did people forget that we didn't lose our coach? Did people forget that three or four players don't make or break a team? I must say, even I was shocked when Damon Duval kicked the 47-yard field goal into a gale-force wind to beat Mississippi State. I really didn't think we were going to win that game, especially with Auburn picked to finish at the bottom of the West. But I knew we had a chance, even in the toughest situations. And one of those was just around the corner.

The following week we were picked to lose to Florida by 21 points. I had been really impressed by Florida in the weeks prior to the game and thought that a 21-point line was more than fair for Auburn. The thought of going to that game sort of gave me a sick feeling. It was supposed to be a nasty weekend, too, with rain and tornadoes. I convinced myself to go by thinking, "You owe it to Auburn after the great win they had the week before against State."

On the way to the game, I just kept thinking that if we could just make a good showing and not get blown out, I would be happy. We got to the game and started looking for tickets. In minutes, we found some for $10 each. My friend said, "That's not good. We must have a bunch of tickets left for them to only be $10."

We later made a bet on how many fans would show for a supposed blow out in the wind and rain. I said over 83,000, and my friend said under. I won a value meal from McDonald's when it was announced that attendance was over 86,000. I was so impressed by the turn out that I almost teared up.

The buzz inside the stadium was unbelievable. We were standing on the upper deck ramp underneath the American Flag as "Tiger", War Eagle VI, came flying by. You could just feel the energy in the air. If somehow Auburn could just get a few breaks, maybe we could win. It seemed crazy to even think this way, but apparently the rest of the fans thought the same thing, because the place was going bananas, and we hadn't even kicked off.

Maybe it was something in the air, or maybe it was holding the Gators to a field goal on their opening drive, but the moment just felt right. On the wings of some inspired defen-

THROUGH THE EYES OF A TIGER

sive play and the coming out party of a new quarterback, Auburn pulled off one of the most SHOCKING upsets in Auburn football history by a final score of 23-20. What makes it so great is that I was there as a tribute to the week before. "Never count the Tigers out" is the lesson I learned that day. The Tigers believed in themselves, and so did 86,000 loyal fans. We had toppled number one. Who could imagine?

WAR EAGLE!

Tim Stanfield
Birmingham, Alabama
Auburn University
Class of 1999

"Auburn vs. Alabama — November 23, 2002"
Tommy Barton, David Kessler and Scott Stanfield

*"How much do you hate this week's enemy?
How much do you want us to win? Will you stand
with me and make noise when they are on offense
to break their concentration? Will you go the extra
mile to a game that we aren't supposed to win?
Will you fly across the country? Will you pull for
Auburn against a high school from Alaska? Will
you encourage our players no matter what? Fair
weather fans aren't acceptable here. I love Auburn
and to all the faithful… War Eagle!"*

– David Kessler

TAKE THAT! 17 – 7!
"Auburn vs. Alabama – November 23, 2002"

I remember as a younger fan that I didn't truly understand the hatred people had for football teams that were not their own. I remember wondering how that happened.

It seemed like many of my friends' conversations centered on what team they hated more. It was almost always because of some experience at a game. And it was almost always a road trip to the enemy territory. I really didn't get it, if you can believe that. I loved going to football games and watching the Tigers, no matter what. I have slowly been becoming a bigger fan because of the people that I most like to watch games with and even being involved with this book.

Looking back, it is not hard for me to see how other teams are hated… downright hated. Go to The Swamp. Go to Death Valley. Hear the taunts. And you will start to feel what I now feel in full force every time. You want to argue with them. You want to give them all the facts of why they are wrong, and how you, not them, pull for the best team there is… the Auburn Tigers.

If diplomacy doesn't work, then it comes down to defending the honor of the school. I can't say it more simply than that. It is hard to outclass people when faced with complete heathens, barbarians at the gate. They want to tear asunder everything that is good and true. Go to Little Rock. Go to Athens. I remember when I started getting it more. Death

Valley. We had all been warned how bad they could get. Crazy Cajuns would just as soon stab and leave you in the swamp somewhere rather than listen to you talk about their beloved Bengal Tigers. I was told not to say anything back, just smile and wave. It is a constant barrage of things yelled at you: "pick a mascot," "war whatever," "are you the eagles?," "we're the real tigers," "you came here to lose," "you should have stayed on Bourbon Street," etc.

After literally hours of abuse, I heard a guy, in the middle of a particularly large group of taunters, yell at me, "I hate elephants." I broke from the code and replied in a yell and a finger pointing, singling him out from the rest of his group, "I do, too!" He stood there, dumbfounded. It never occurred to this idiot that we have more than one school in our state. I certainly started to understand what it meant to just despise some people.

Somehow, I had never managed to go to an Auburn–Alabama game. It really killed me. I had gone to many other games, and I had tried so many times to get into "the game." But even when I went to school there, the game was an away game, and I didn't get the ticket in time. I had asked for a ticket as a Christmas present for several years, but that never seemed to happen. Later, I would try to get one from a scalper year after year. I just never had enough for what they were asking. I never seemed to have the right connection to get someone to pull one for me. Believe me, it's tough being outside of Jordan-Hare Stadium, hearing the crowd, hearing the band. Your standing in darkness on the concrete, and you can look up and see the beautiful light going straight up over the rim of the stadium into the night sky. But you simply don't have enough money to go inside. You didn't plan well enough for it. You sulk away to some bar to watch the game on a TV. And trust me, there is no consolation in being one of the first people at Toomer's after the comeback win in 1997.

I could have gone in 2000. There certainly were plenty of tickets from the fickle Alabama crowds whose team was hurting, especially, after being picked preseason third in the country and finishing the season with only three wins. But I was already sick, and couldn't risk getting into the freezing rain and sleet that came down on the crowd all day. In hindsight, it would have been worth being sick to go and see that game.

My story really begins in 2001. I had a good job and was able to save a lot of money. It really didn't matter to me this time. I was going to pay whatever to get into that game. Auburn was riding high, and I was going for broke to get in. I can't stress this enough; there was no way I wasn't going. I got a ticket and thought to myself, "finally, I'm going in. I'm going to see it."

You know, I can't remember one detail of it, with the exception of Cadillac rumbling forward on three carries in the opening minutes and amassing a huge number of yards. I thought we are going to kill them if that was the pace we set all day. Then Cadillac was hurt. I can't believe anything except that it was intentional. Alabama had recruited him so hard, and I knew many people who were sore about the fact that he chose Auburn. You can't convince me that in the very first time he played them, he gets hurt on his fourth carry and there wasn't foul play? I don't believe it.

I remember being in a sort of haze after the game. I was walking by myself in no particular direction. My friends were nowhere around, and I don't think I even noticed or cared. I walked by a guy decked out in Alabama garb, and he was stomping on an Auburn shaker. He was just pulverizing it into the concrete of the sidewalk. I got about four steps past him in my daze, and it really hit me what he was doing… The fact was he was doing this to a piece of plastic. But that plastic shaker represented the whole of the campus he was standing in. I stopped… turned around… and anger started to take me over. I could envision what I would do. I would walk back and act as though I was bending over to pick up the shaker when I would come up, take him off his feet and full body tackle him to the ground and commence to treating him like that shaker. It would leave me open as I bent over, but this kid wouldn't dare infuriate me anymore.

Standing there, staring at him, he noticed me suddenly, and with a flash of fear across his face, remembered where he was and who surrounded him as far as the eye could see. He froze and stood there staring back at me. He had some friends standing behind him that were Auburn fans, and I gave them a sideways glance. They gave me a look as if to say, "Yeah, we're pretty tired of it, too. If you want to, go ahead." I took two steps towards him when a good Auburn man and his Auburn girl walked by me. I was so focused that I hadn't seen them at all. He put his hand on my shoulder as he walked by. He patted it twice and said, "It's okay. We'll get them next year."

That was really all it took. I came back to my senses and wasn't in the daze anymore. I was on Thatch Avenue. I was right next to Cary Hall where I had taken Environmental Biology and was more aware of my surroundings. I don't think he could grasp how lucky he was as I turned and walked away.

The next year was a different story. Auburn was a beat up team. The week before losing to Georgia in a gut-wrenching game that can only be described as the same lucky catch USC had made, the same lucky catch Florida had made, and now Georgia had made that same catch. Luck. Not skill. I had heard it plenty before, "Sometimes it's better to be lucky than good," and in my opinion, we should have had one loss at this point in the year. You always love the movie ending of a hated team losing in the last seconds, but these instances had been us losing in the last seconds, and it was hard for me that whole next week. Alabama, on the other hand, was riding high. It seemed as though Coach Dennis Franchione had them set to do really well once they got off probation. All of their players had stayed through coach changes and probation. They all bought into what he sold them.

Auburn, on the other hand, would be using our fourth string running back, Tre Smith. He was basically untested in college. I can only speak for myself, but I'm used to having a big back, a guy who just clobbers other guys, or guys that count their YAC (yards after contact) yards and use that as a selling point for themselves. I actually felt bad for Tre. I remember thinking, "here is a guy who is going to go through a true trial by fire. He was going to be baptized into college football against a team that deliberately goes out to hurt people. Go ahead and stick a fork in him."

And Cooper Wallace was in, too. Now Cooper had really stood out to me at the A-Day game, but that seemed like a century ago now. Who knows how he would play? It certainly had to be in his head that he was getting his first start when everything was on the line. How can that not mess with you mentally? Any Alabama fan you came across would tell you shortly we had no chance going into this game.

And I was again in a position of not having enough money, especially to find one of the hard to come across Auburn away tickets… much less an Alabama fan who didn't want to watch their team beat up on an under-gunned Auburn team, at home. I had convinced myself that I didn't want to go. It would be too painful to scrape up the money of some exorbitant scalped price just to see them lose again.

But there is one thing that is true, always true. If I have a ticket... I go. I don't care if it's in Alaska playing a high school that has ringers from the pros. I go. I got the call on Friday that I not only had a ticket with my name on it, but it was freely given. All skepticism went away instantly. If I had felt like I didn't think we would win, that was just my mind preparing me for not having a ticket. Now that I had one, I was excited, really excited. I started thinking of redemption. I want to win, and I want to be there. I think the people at work couldn't believe the turn around in my personality after I hung up that phone. They knew what a big fan I was, especially after going to Los Angeles for the USC game, and they had been leaving me alone and steering clear of me all week. I honestly think they just wanted me to get through the week so I could concentrate again. Now it was as if I couldn't shut up.

The next day I went to see The Auburn Tigers play at Bryant-Denny Stadium. I hadn't been to a game in Tuscaloosa and was struck by the differences. We got there fairly early and paid to park in the back yard of a house that was many city blocks from the stadium. That may be the first time I have had to pay to park at a game on a campus before. I would expect to pay at Legion Field. I expect to pay at the Georgia dome, but not in Tuscaloosa. I remember just thinking how terrible that place was. That just irked me right from the start.

The first thing I needed to do was use the bathroom. I set out to find one. I walked back to 15th Street, close to the bridge that goes to the older part of Tuscaloosa. The first two places

I went in kicked me out. The third place was a beauty shop. So when I walked in, it was like someone pulled the needle across a record to stop the music. I was a guy, and I was a guy dressed in all orange. I bet they didn't see that everyday. I asked if I could use the bathroom. They only said, "We normally charge $4.00, but since you're an Auburn fan, it'll be $10.00." I just said, "Fine thank you," and went straight in. What can I say? They didn't kick me out like the first two places did.

When I walked back out I had the money in my hand and went up to the lady that said it and offered it to her. I was thinking all the while the story I would tell to anyone that would listen about the greedy thieves that were the hated Alabama faithful. She turned it down and said she had been joking. She cut up with me for a moment, and I actually felt better about being there.

I proceeded to walk out, when a younger, arrogant girl at the front counter stopped me and said, "Where is my 10 bucks?" I told her how the lady said that it was ok and let me go. She replied, "I don't care what she told you. You owe me ten bucks." With that, she leaned forward and stuck out her hand and glared at me. I slowly reached in my pocket, grabbed the $10 bill and started to pull it out. I was thinking how wrong I had been to trust them, how wrong I was to let my guard down for even a moment. She obviously saw my reaction to her telling me that I still owed her and asked, "You know you're here to lose right?" I said, "what?" in disbelief that she could be this brazen. The money is now in my hand out stretched to her. She took this opportunity to really push my patience by saying, "Keep your money, but I want you to say that you know you are here to lose." (A more spiteful girl I couldn't imagine.) I took a moment. Considered my options and replied with the nicest face I could muster, I said, "Good luck to you today."

With that, she erupted in laughter. She laughed, and other women in the shop joined her. She said as she was elbowing another lady, in between laughs and gasps for air, "Luck! We don't need luck. Did you hear what he said?"

I walked out with a renewed anger towards them. I was recounting the moments from the year before. The kid on the sidewalk. Their constant arrogance. I remembered how confident we had been the year before. I was positive we would win that game and we hadn't. I said a small prayer and just wanted it to be even. I wanted them to know the feeling of despair, the kind of despair that follows a crestfallen cockiness of a sure thing, just as I had felt the year before. And I wanted her to know it most of all.

When I got back to the group, they were all having fun, and I was just quiet. I couldn't speak for a little while because I was so angry. I really couldn't imagine having fun in Tuscaloosa. I was so focused on what in my mind had been a congressional "declaration of war." It did take me quite a while, but I slowly started becoming myself again. We tailgated and threw the football. I ran into some friends of mine and talked with them some, swapping "how great would it be 'ifs'" and just having a good time. But rest assured, any Bama fan I saw from then on I couldn't help but glare at. They were the enemy, and I was behind enemy lines.

Our number had dwindled down to two of us. Just Scott and myself remained at the tailgate spot as kickoff neared. Everyone needed to go meet whoever and had left us there. Scott turns to me and he says, "Tell me what 'Budweiser' stands for, and we will win today." Now this was some dumb joke he had told me at another game weeks ago, but for some reason it became very serious. I mean, I really thought it was true, buying into the whole omen superstition. I immediately snapped out, "Because yoU Deserve What Every Individual Enjoys Regularly." But I left out the "s." What was the "s?" I had no idea. I went through it again. It makes a complete sentence?!?! What else doesn't it say? Panic started to set in, and he was looking at me as if I wanted us to lose or something. He started giving me hints. And I honestly laugh every time I think of this, but it was so utterly important at that moment. I kept wishing he had said we would win if I could name the offensive and defensive line. Anything that would have been easier than some obscure joke from what seemed like months ago. "Should!" "Should," I shouted, as loud as I could without drawing attention to the dumb game we were playing… "Because yoU Deserve What Every Individual Should Enjoy Regularly." We both laughed for a minute, and I said, "Are you ready to go yet?" So we left.

On the way to meet up with everyone it struck me again how terrible this place was. They had street venders set up on the road going to the game as if it was City Stages or some kind of third world country, but instead of fish hanging on a hook, they had stuffed elephants and checkered hats. I couldn't help but think how trashy this place was. No place I had been to was like this. Venice Beach, maybe, but even that was nicer. They reminded me of carnies at a fair trying to sell you some cheap prize that you would almost instantly wonder why you had bought it because now you were stuck with it throughout the game.

We met up with everyone right outside of the "will-call" booth. As we were getting everything together and ready to go in, we were forced to listen to the jeers of their fans. But here we were taking a few jabs back at them. One guy had a sign that simply read, "Jason Campbell vs. the $650,000 line." I was dying at that. I remember Lou Holtz saying something to the effect that Alabama was a good team. No one gets NCAA sanctions for recruiting bad players.

We went in and squeezed into the Auburn section. Our tickets were all over the place but we wanted to stay together. We asked if it would be ok if we stood near some people, and they said it was fine. We all crowded in together, double stacked in the space of a single seat.

We ended up in the end zone right next to the tunnel where the Tigers came out. The Alabama fans were just on the other side of this tunnel, and they were being so loud and obnoxious that it blew even me away. And it really was like war all during the game. That tunnel even started to have the properties of a moat or trench for the DMZ. The field was filled with people. Band members, dance team and cheer-leaders were all going as hard as they could. Then Scott tells us he has a first half jinx bet on them. The principle of a jinx bet is simple. If you are a guy who loses bets... bet on the team you want to lose. Usually this is the team that is playing Auburn. The trick is, Wayne had told me in the past, bet enough so that it hurts you a little. If you have plenty of money, that won't work, but if $20 is a significant amount of money like, say, all the money your wife would give you for lunch the next week. Well, that's some hurt. Scott had $60 on Alabama in the first half with a line of like 7 and a half points. I told him I would take $20 from him, and Tim said he would take $20. Now we all had a jinx on these checkered-hat-loving fools. They never expected the next half of football.

Kickoff. The ball went to Roderick Hood, and he dropped the ball.

I felt my heart stop. It wasn't the worst-case scenario for a start, but it was close behind it. We started out first and 10 on our 11. We had a long way to go. Tre gets the hand off the very next play and ran forward nine yards. The whole time I kept thinking to myself... don't get hurt... please don't get hurt... if he gets hurt, they are going to have to put in a trainer as our running back!

That run set up a great fake reminiscent of David George from Georgia in the 2001 game. Tre pulled it off. Campbell pulled it off. They bit. And the very next thing I know, we are on their side of the 50 on their 29-yard line. And, we have spent exactly one minute of the game clock. We were so excited, I couldn't see the field for five minutes, so many people were jumping in front of me in the cramped space.

We didn't score on that drive. We should have. The very next play was a throw to the corner of the end zone, and it looked like we had it. That drive didn't end in points, but it did end in confidence. And that was exactly what they didn't want to give us. They got the ball, and whatever they did, they had penalties to negate more than half of it. They did get across the 50, which was rare, looking back.

Then we got the ball back, and this time Tre stood up and seemed to say, "Get a load of me!" The very first play he goes 52 yards in 12 seconds, to their 16-yard line. Cooper had a huge block on the free safety, and the whole offensive line just seemed to open the door and say, "go ahead Tre. We've got these guys." I can't express the excitement. We were down there. In an instant, we had taken the ball back over on downs and were even closer than we had been to the goal line before. Robert Johnson scored two plays later. We couldn't believe it. Later when at home and watching the TIVO recording of the game, the announcers said this is the first time Alabama has trailed since they lost to Georgia. Another great Omen!

The very next drive it was Tre and Ben Obomanu, and then it ended up with 17 to 87 again. Robert Johnson got his second touchdown of the day with the help of a great pass from Campbell. We were just going nuts. The whole Auburn section was going crazy. I couldn't believe that this is what I was witnessing. I kept checking the scoreboard over and over. It continued to read 14-0. I was looking back to my friends. We were all in shock and awe. This was truly the best start to a game I had ever seen, and it was all in the first quarter.

The second quarter it appeared that they made some adjustments. We ended up with a field goal courtesy of Damon Duval, and the score was now 17-0. As half time was approaching and the clock just seemed to be winding down, I realized how excited we were and how dumbfounded all of the 'Bama fans were. I tapped Tim and said, "Is that the best $20 bucks you ever spent or what?" He agreed that he could think of nothing in the world better, and we both gave Scott the money. Then came half time.

I remember the silence as the game came to the half. I'm no mind reader, but you could see it in their faces. You could feel it in the air. They were scared they wouldn't score a point in the game. It had been talked about so much, that they had never scored a point on Auburn in Bryant-Denny Stadium. A friend had pointed out to me that Auburn and Central Florida were the only two undefeated teams at Bryant-Denny. And they still are. They had that sinking feeling of despair I mentioned. They were miserable because of it, and I was reveling in it.

It was quiet... not like it had been with the pompous and boisterousness of all of their fans at the beginning of the game. That was gone. The band and the cheerleaders reminded me of the cheerleaders at a UAB game in their first

THROUGH THE EYES OF A TIGER

couple of seasons... trying to get people fired up when they are hopeless is the hardest thing in the world. I thought of that girl at the beauty shop. I wondered if she was still at work and how my, "good luck to you today," must be ringing in her ears.

The second half was just a battle. Alabama did finally score. It only took three centuries, but they did manage it. Another friend mused that maybe in a few more centuries they might be able to win there.

The game came to a close and it was amazing. We all started dancing and just going crazy. There was a nice lady that was right next to us, and I gave her a hug. She hugged right back without the slightest thought about not knowing me from Adam. I asked her to take some pictures of us.

We climbed down to the walkway that was just above the field. We were there as the players came back out and were giving us high fives. The flag was circling on the field as different people were taking turns carrying it. Scott was right in front of me, and he was bending all the way over shaking hands with one of the players. Ben Obomanu was standing directly in front of me about five feet away. He shot his wristband up towards us. I grabbed it and put it on. It's still on my mantle to this day.

After quite a while, we went down into the bowels of the stadium, and I found myself yelling, "We own this stadium. We just took out a second mortgage on it."

We went to meet the players coming out of the stadium, and we bought the flyers that had the fresh score on it. We ended up back at the car, and it was amazing. It was as if there wasn't an Alabama fan in Tuscaloosa. We waited out the traffic a little while. We continued to tailgate and call everyone we knew on our cell phones. I painted on the back of my car a big, "Say our name!" Since Coach Franchione always called Auburn that school down the road and would never call Auburn by her name. I didn't realize then that it wouldn't matter if he ever did in a few short weeks.

We ended up back in Birmingham and at Bell Bottoms'. Wayne told me to tell him the score as often as I could to remind him of it. It became a Pavlovian response. I would catch his eye, yell, "17 to 7!" and he would dance with the kind of happiness that can only come from crushing the dreams of your greatest rival. We stayed out all night. I remember going to Arby's really late and asking them if they had any of the Tommy Tuberville bobble heads left. They had four. I bought them up and gave them out immediately.

It has been a while now. I still like to text message my friends a nice "17 to 7" every once in a while. When I got a new cell phone, I picked my last four digits as 1727… just a little nod to a great day. There is a part of me that likes these little things that remind me of a great victory over the hated Crimson Tide. And there is another part of me that hates that I trivialize it like that. It was a truly special day and will always remain so.

All in all, I want to thank the players and the coaches. I can only enjoy the happiness that they provide. To the "Bammers" in the world, I want you to know that every time you say the "storied Crimson Tide," I say, " the hated Crimson Tide." Every time you say, "the University," I will say, "the University of Alabama at Tuscaloosa, not to be confused with the Universities of Alabama at Birmingham, Huntsville or West Alabama (Livingston)." Every time you call us a "cow college" or "the barn," I will take pride knowing that the techniques that are developed at Auburn for growing food benefits everyone. I don't remember anyone ever thinking the world was a better place because it had more lawyers.

I want to make sure that we don't get overconfident like them. Anybody can have their worst game when some one else is having their best. Anyone else can be a pompous fool yelling the same things that all the rest of their fans say, over and over. To the Tigers, I say just keep your head down and do what you do. Don't listen to the hype that everyone is just dying to get you mixed up with. Walk the walk and forget about all the talk. To my fellow fans, I want to tell them one thing, "I question your hatred." How much do you hate this week's enemy? How much do you want us to win? Will you stand with me and make noise when they are on offense to break their concentration? Will you go the extra mile to a game that we aren't supposed to win? Will you fly across the country? Will you pull for Auburn against a high school from Alaska? Will you encourage our players no matter what? Fair weather fans aren't acceptable here. I love Auburn and to all the faithful… War Eagle!

David Kessler
Birmingham, Alabama

GO TO AUBURN,
BE FOREVER CHANGED

I have descended into college football's Grand Canyon. I have stood in its Alps. I have gazed at its ocean sunset. I have done all of these things and I've been changed forever.

I knew, of course, that we were different up here. I understood that autumn Saturdays in our burg have never been given over to any kind of serious sporting fervor. I've accepted for a good, long while that a fair amount of our citizens regularly choose to pick apples or seal driveways rather than head to the Carrier Dome to watch the Syracuse University Orangemen at play.

But, Lord have mercy on our college football souls, I've come to realize we're not merely quirky in these parts. And we're not just overly particular. No, having attended a game in Auburn, Ala. – which is like going to Mass in Rome – I'm convinced that, by comparison, we're as dead as the flying wedge.

"Let me tell you something," said Paul Pasqualoni, the SU coach who can recognize bedlam when he is forced to shout above it. "Being in that stadium with all those people - the noise level, the atmosphere - was exciting. It was a lot of fun. To me, it was just spectacular being there."

He was speaking of Jordan-Hare Stadium, where four days earlier his SU club had lost to the Auburn Tigers 37-34 in an environment that was equal parts Woodstock, Mardi Gras, New Year's Eve and Madonna's last wedding. And the Crimson Tide boys, those rascals from the other side of the state, weren't even in town, to say nothing of the Bulldogs, Gators or Razorbacks.

Nah, it was just the Orangemen, a non-league bunch from somewhere up north... with a losing record yet. But it didn't matter. This, because the cherished Tigers were on the other side, and that was enough for those Alabama locals to respond the way the French did when Patton's army showed up in Paris.

"I missed my wife's birthday so I could cheer on my beloved alma mater against Syracuse," Brent Miller wrote in an e-mail addressed to me following the three-overtime affair. "But you know what? I would have been there if our opponent had been the state of New York's worst high school team."

"Country, God and college football are usually our top three passions," e-mailed another Auburn guy, Steve Fleming. "But not always in that order."

"I grew up in Denver in a family with season tickets to the Broncos games," e-mailed yet another believer, Rick Pavek. "I call Auburn home now and, take my word for this, Broncomania is nothing like Tigermania."

The point is, with the Orangemen returning to the gray Dome that is so often lifeless to play Big East Conference foe Pittsburgh on Saturday, it's clear that somebody's not getting it. Either the Auburn faithful – and people like them in Knoxville and South Bend and Lincoln and Gainesville and

Columbus and Austin and elsewhere - are far too crazed or we're way too cool.

Listen, down there in eastern Alabama they pass out full-color, high-gloss, 22-by-17-inch, two-sided, fold-out pamphlets titled, "The 2002 Guide To Game Day At Auburn University." And on Page 2 of each can be found the announcement that nobody is allowed to begin tailgating until 4 p.m. the day before the game.

"You can't be anything but envious," said Jake Crouthamel, the Syracuse athletic director who was a wide-eyed witness to all of the SU-Auburn doings. "You can't be anything but envious when you have that kind of support. I mean, there were 84,000 people in the seats. And the RVs and house trailers were lined up five miles outside of town. When you talk about the epitome of what the college football experience is all about ... that's it. Auburn is the epitome. You couldn't possibly be unaware of the spectacle, even if you were trying to be unaware."

The orange-clad zealots, who are in their seats fully 30 minutes prior to kickoff, thunder through choreographed cheers. The band, which is saluted upon its arrival by the big house with a standing ovation, blares. The PA system, which continuously blasts the sounds of a growling tiger, pipes in songs by the Dixie Chicks and interviews with the Auburn coaches.

Before the game, there is the great Tiger Walk during which the Auburn players march along Donahue Street through thousands of people, some of whom weep, and into the stadium. After the game, there is the mass papering of famous Toomer's Corner downtown. And between all of that, a golden eagle circles the place before landing on the field to a deafening roar.

And us? Um, let's see. We can't fill 49,000 seats. We debate, ad nauseam, standing-vs.-sitting in the Dome. We give our tickets to takers at the door who had to be schooled in the art of courtliness. We regularly vacate the joint long before the final gun. We allow, in a good-idea-gone-bad, a bunch of vulgar louts planted in a thing called "The O-Zone" to chant expressions you'd never say in front of Mom at the dinner table.

In other words to compare our college football experience to that of Auburn (and a lot of other places) is to compare a skillet of beans to a plate of Chilean sea bass. And while that might sound harsh, it doesn't make the words any less true.

Believe me on this. Please. I have descended into college football's Grand Canyon. I have stood in its Alps. I have gazed at its ocean sunset. I have attended a game at Jordan-Hare Stadium in Auburn, Alabama. And I've been changed forever.

Bud Poliquin,
Post-Standard Columnist
Syracuse, NY

"Cheer on the Tigers… Rain or Shine"
Auburn vs. LSU - October 26, 2002
Cary Murray and Kristen Stone

*"I remembered that those long nights spent
cramming also typically included a
study-break trip to the Flush, the ice cream
shop that my roommate's mother's
mother went to when she was at Auburn."*

— Kristen Stone

MOVING FORWARD

We've all heard the old saying that in order to move forward, we must first leave something behind, but I never truly realized what that meant until the day I left Auburn.

Crossing the Georgia-Alabama state line after graduation was the beginning of a new and unknown life for me, and a real "catch 22." On one hand I was thrilled with the prospect of not having to stay up all night cramming for a six-chapter exam or having to miss Mel and the Party Hats at the Supper Club to finish that 3,000-word essay that was due the next day.

The idea of working only eight hours a day... with no homework... didn't sound so bad. And then there was the paycheck. I savored the idea that every two weeks someone would hand me a small rectangular document that would contain more than my bank account saw during my entire senior year at college.

Then, reality set in, and I realized the other half of the "catch 22," the part that involves leaving something behind. And that something was Auburn. I remembered that those long nights spent cramming typically included a study-break trip to the "Flush," the ice cream shop that my roommate's mother's mother went to when she was at Auburn. I remembered that, after I turned in my essay, I had a whole group of friends around to help me celebrate my accomplishment. I realized that my time at Auburn had been far more than a mere academic experience. The entire campus had been my class-room, and my education was made complete by all the people who shared that great place with me ... my Auburn family. I learned some of life's most precious lessons there.

I know that I am not alone in feeling that a part of me will always miss Auburn desperately. Yet, I know that it is this longing that makes homecomings at Auburn priceless. A night at the Supper Club means so much more than just "going out;" it's a walk down "Memory Lane."

Football games are a brand new experience. Sure, I sit with the same people and wave that same orange and blue shaker, yelling the same "WAR EAGLE" as Tiger soars through the sky. But now I notice more. I really hear the roar of Jordan-Hare Stadium, brimming with some 86,000 proud Auburn fans. I know I can count on the AU band to play the cherished Alma Mater at the end of each game, regardless of the outcome. I savor the smell of hotdogs mixed with bourbon. I feel an overwhelming rush of emotion when I hear "Eye of the Tiger" and the orange and blue take the field. At this moment, amidst all this excitement, I realize that no matter where life takes me and how my world may change, there will always be a constant in my life: Auburn.

I know that, years from now, I can return to the Plains, and it will be just as it's always been. Haley Center will still be the tallest building in Lee County, and Samford Hall will still play the sweet sounds of the fight song every hour on the hour. I know that the people walking the campus uphold the values and virtues of the Auburn family, as others will for genera-tions to come. I know that the greeting of choice is still "War Eagle," and I relish the fact that people from other places still don't quite understand exactly what it means, or why we say it. I know that every so often the heavens will reflect a true Auburn sunset of fiery orange and brilliant blue. And I know that this is my Auburn; it will never change.

War Eagle!

Kristen Stone
Atlanta, Georgia
Auburn University
Class of 1999

FANtastic Memories, LLC.
Tim Stansfield, Illia Ayers, David Kessler and Mark Stanfield

STORY BEHIND THE BOOK

This book was at first a twinkle in Tim Stanfield's eye in 1999. Upon graduating from Auburn University, two things seemed essential in his mind: give something back to his Alma Mater and rally the fans. He had always loved the fact that the Auburn University Bookstore had a policy stating any book written by an Alumni was automatically included on their shelves. He knew he wanted to be counted among those authors.

Later in 2000, Tim, David Kessler, and contingent of other friends traveled to Logan Martin Lake for an afternoon outing. A great time was shared cooking out, eating and just having fun. It wasn't very long before the group had gathered around a campfire and were reminiscing stories of the glory days. It was not odd for this group that most of the great experiences shared in these stories had ties to Auburn in some form or fashion. They told of great road trips, campus romance and amazing athletic feats.

A few short days passed when Tim asked David if he had enjoyed sharing those old stories. David enthusiastically responded, "How could anyone not love those stories?" Tim then shared his revelation about a book that was a collection of great Auburn stories. Tim defined it as "tailgating in book form." Needless to say, David bought into the concept.

Not long after, Tim asked his brother, Mark Stanfield and good friend Illia Ayers about the concept and they agreed that it was a great idea. Almost instantly, Illia had his late night revelation of the title and called Tim at 2:45 a.m. to share it. A name like this just couldn't wait until the morning. All agreed that, "Through the Eyes of a Tiger," embodied the meaning of the goal they wanted to accomplish. With the name in place, Tim, David, Mark and Illia set sail to accomplish their task. Ideas were tossed for a few months, followed by weekly meetings termed "organizational meetings". Keep in mind that not one of the four had any experience in writing, editing, or publishing. Determining how to proceed to create the book was very different in each of their "eyes", but two things were certain: Their goal was to unite all Auburn fans and create a perpetual forum to share the Auburn experience. These Auburn Men recognized that it was possible to create a "movement" that will continue on, honoring Auburn University. Through the Eyes of a Tiger, "A Book by the Auburn Fans... For Auburn Fans."

Thanks and WAR EAGLE !!!

FANtastic Memories, LLC

THROUGH THE EYES OF A TIGER SUPPORTERS

"Birmingham-Jefferson County Auburn Club
Golf Tournament – May 13, 2003"
FANtastic Memories, LLC with Coach Tuberville

Illia Ayers, David Kessler, Tommy Tuberville,
Mark Stanfield and Tim Stanfield

In its infancy, Through the Eyes of a Tiger© was the dream of four everyday Auburn fans. We worked very hard developing the concept and organizing our efforts. The result of this effort was the incorporation of FANtastic Memories, LLC. Realizing that we were operating on limited resources, we proceeded with faith that Through the Eyes of a Tiger© would create a movement that others would appreciate and support.

THROUGH THE EYES OF A TIGER SUPPORTERS

Indeed, FANtastic Memories, LLC has received the very generous support of businesses and individuals, making our dream financially attainable. We are very appreciative of these sponsors who believed in Through the Eyes of a Tiger© and FANtastic Memories, LLC. In turn, we hope that you will take the opportunity to thank the businesses listed on the next few pages and support them with your patronage.

WEDDINGS BY JILL

Floral, Consulting, Accessories

1834 West Fifth Street
Montgomery, AL 36106
334.356.2933
www.weddingsbyjill.com

AYERS PHOTOGRAPHY

*Weddings, Portraits, Events
Custom Portraiture*

Yuri Ayers
Hoover, Alabama
205.823.9519
yuriayers@earthlink.com

REALTYSOUTH LAURA STANFIELD

Jefferson and Shelby County

(c) 205.601.7837
(w) 205.879.3636
laurastanfield.realtysouth.com
lstanfield@realtysouth.com

BLACK DESIGN ARCHITECTURE

Lance Black, A.I.A.

Birmingham, Alabama
Phone 205.868.6921
Fax 205-868-6922
lbarch@bellsouth.net

KOSKI CONSTRUCTION

David and Joe Koski

Birmingham, Alabama
205.823.0106

THROUGH THE EYES OF A TIGER SUPPORTERS

MONTGOMERY MALL

2925-A Montgomery Mall
Montgomery, Alabama 36116
334.284.1533
montgomerymallshopping.com

REALTYSOUTH

Jefferson and Shelby County

Amber Curran
(vm) 205.327.8410
(m) 205.365.8454
ambersellsnewhomes.com
amcurran@realtysouth.com

Wanda Davis
(vm) 205.244.0641
(m) 205.365.0991
wandadavis.com
wdavis@realtysouth

UNIVERSITY INN

129 North College Street
Auburn, AL 36830
Call Brandi
334.821.4632
334.826.3394

Escape to
BLUE SPRING MANOR

Stop in for a stay & remember us for your stay on game-day

Ray and Doris Harris
205.672.9955
www.bluespringmanor.com

KATHY WESTBROOK

America's Best Selling Brand

Mary Kay Independent
Sales Director
205.822.9877
marykay.com/kathywestbrook

THROUGH THE EYES OF A TIGER SUPPORTERS

DISCOUNT TOBACCO WORLD

1907 South College Street
Auburn, AL 36832
334.466.2137

1437 Fox Run Parkway
Opelika, AL 36801
334.741.8908

Birmingham – Alexander City – Childersburg
Bessemer - Helena - Pell City

MAX TOOL, INC. - CARBIDE DEPOT

1474 Pettyjohn Road
Bessemer, Alabama 35022
205.942.2466
Toll free: 800.783.6298
www.maxtoolinc.com

BENNETT'S SPORTS CAFE

Altadena Square, 4704-C
Cahaba River Road
Bham, AL 35234
205.967.0018

ICE CREAM CLUB

Highway 31
Vestavia Hills, Alabama 3216
205.822.7957

War Eagle !

GLOBAL CHAMPIONSHIP WRESTLING

www.gcwpro.com
www.vinnyv.com
gcwpro@yahoo.com

ALAGASCO

An Energen Company

20 South 20th Street
Birmingham, AL 35203
205.326.8200
www.alagasco.com

THROUGH THE EYES OF A TIGER SUPPORTERS

240

THROUGH THE EYES OF A TIGER SUPPORTERS

THROUGH THE EYES OF A TIGER SUPPORTERS

Momma Goldberg's Deli

The Auburn Hotel & Dixon Conference Center

StillWaters Golf Resort

Auburn Links at Millcreek Golf Course

Limestone Springs Golf Course

Highland Golf Course

AuburnFootball.com

Best Western Auburn

Cherokee Run Golf Club

Eagle Point Golf Course

Indian Pines Golf Course

Goose Pond Colony Golf Course

Dauphine Isle Golf Course

Chesley Oaks Golf Course

Bellezza Day Spa

FarmLinks Golf Course

The Meadows Golf Course

THROUGH THE EYES OF A TIGER SUPPORTERS

Bill and Elissa Alldredge

Emma Aycock

Robert Ballard

Brett W. Barnett

Carrie Brown

Merideth Burleson

Cortnie Cotton

Katie Dubois

Sandra Ewell

David Ferrell

Hal and Ginger Ferrell

Jack Ginn

Ginger Glenn

Pam Griffin

Mark Griggs

Kenny Hawsey

Charles Heaton

Samantha Higginbotham

Ashley Hudson

Stacey Inzina

Mary Claire Janiga

John and Catherine Kessler

Joyce Kessler

Paul Koury

Jim Lawson

Jason Lee

Pat and Debbie Lorino

Julie Massey

David McWaters

Michael Melvin

Heather Moffett

Randi Moore

Royce Morris

Beth Morrow

Lonnie and June Pardue

Lee Parker

Rodd Parrish

Richard Rohn

Robin Salze

Rudy and Carolyn Schaffer

Jackie Sims

Carol Smith

Jerry Spurlock

Alan and Barbara Stanfield

Wayne and Laura Stanfield

Sandy Tombrello

Don Utz

Arthur Wade

Nelson Wade

Kay Waid

Kathy Weaver

Justin and Shannon Wesley

Lance Wood

Sheree York

Steve York

AUTHOR INDEX

FUTURE BOOK INFORMATION

We Sincerely Hope That You Have Enjoyed Reading
THROUGH THE EYES OF A TIGER©
"A Book By Auburn Fans… For Auburn Fans"

Please know that the 2nd Edition is already underway.

DO YOU HAVE A GREAT AUBURN MEMORY TO SHARE?

If so, please submit your story or story concept in writing
to our website or by mail. If your story is not complete,
that's OK. FANtastic Memories, LLC will assist you in
your developing your thoughts and memories into
the perfect Auburn Story.

VISIT OUR WEBSITE AT:

WWW.4AU2.COM

E-MAIL YOUR STORY: MARK@4AU2.COM

OR

MAIL TO:

THROUGH THE EYES OF A TIGER
P.O. BOX 660582
BIRMINGHAM, AL 35266

QUICK ORDER FORM

Email orders: order@4au2.com

Telephone orders: 205.823.6988 or 205.427.8486

Postal orders: Through the Eyes of a Tiger,
P.O. Box 660582, Birmingham, AL 35266

Website orders: www.4au2.com

....

THROUGH THE EYES OF A TIGER

Number of copies: _____ @ $19.95 each + $1.60 each (8% Sales Tax if in Alabama

Shipping/Handling: $4 for first book ($2 each additional)

Total: _____

Name: _____

Address: _____

City:_____ Zip: _____

Phone: _____

Email Address: _____

      Payment: ☐ Check   ☐ Visa   ☐ MC   ☐ AmEx

Card Number: _____

Name on Card: _____ Exp. date:_____